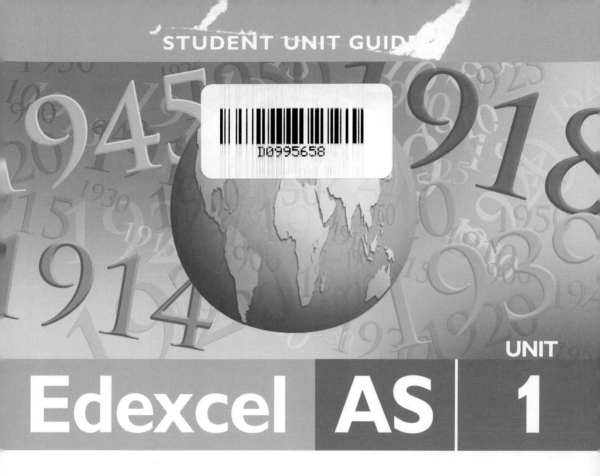

STUDENT UNIT GUIDE

UNIT

Edexcel AS 1

History

Stalin's Russia, 1924–53 (Option D4)

Robin Bunce and Laura Gallagher

Series Editor: Derrick Murphy

Philip Allan Updates, an imprint of Hodder Education, an Hachette UK company, Market Place, Deddington, Oxfordshire OX15 0SE

Orders
Bookpoint Ltd, 130 Milton Park, Abingdon, Oxfordshire OX14 4SB
tel: 01235 827827
fax: 01235 400401
e-mail: education@bookpoint.co.uk
Lines are open 9.00 a.m.–5.00 p.m., Monday to Saturday, with a 24-hour message answering service. You can also order through the Philip Allan Updates website: www.philipallan.co.uk

ISBN 978-0-340-99044-5

First printed 2009
Impression number 5 4 3
Year 2014 2013 2012

This guide has been written specifically to support students preparing for the Edexcel AS History Unit 1 examination. The content has been neither approved nor endorsed by Edexcel and remains the sole responsibility of the authors.

Typeset by DC Graphic Design, Swanley Village, Kent
Printed by MPG Books, Bodmin

Hachette UK's policy is to use papers that are natural, renewable and recyclable products and made from wood grown in sustainable forests. The logging and manufacturing processes are expected to conform to the environmental regulations of the country of origin.

Contents

Introduction

■ ■ ■

Content Guidance

■ ■ ■

Questions and Answers

Introduction

Aims of the unit

Unit 1 is worth 25% of the A-level course or 50% of the AS. The unit requires knowledge of the topic and the ability to explain historical events and assess their significance in the wider context. There are no sources on the exam paper, so source skills are not necessary.

You are required to provide clear information that directly answers the question. In addition examiners are looking for detailed and precise supporting evidence and examples to demonstrate that your statements are accurate. These examples need to be linked clearly to the argument.

You will have 40 minutes to write an answer to each question in the exam. In this time it is difficult to address every issue of some relevance to the question. Examiners will therefore award full marks for answers that deal adequately and in detail with most of the central issues.

Please note **Stalin's Russia, 1924–53** is Topic D4 of Paper 6HI01/D, A World Divided: Communism and Democracy in the Twentieth Century. You will need to be prepared for at least two topics from Option D, and in the exam you will be required to answer questions relating to two different topics. This book deals exclusively with Topic D4: Stalin's Russia, 1924–53.

The examination paper

The exam paper has seven topics, and each topic contains two questions. You are required to answer questions on two topics. Within each topic you must choose one question only.

The format of the topic questions in a typical examination paper is as follows:

> **6HI01/D — A World Divided: Communism and Democracy in the Twentieth Century**
>
> **Answer TWO questions: ONE question on each of the TWO topics for which you have been prepared. You may only answer ONE question on each topic.**
>
> **D4 — Stalin's Russia, 1924–53**
>
> **EITHER**
>
> **7.** Why did...   **(Total: 30 marks)**
>
> **OR**
>
> **8.** How far...   **(Total: 30 marks)**

Examinable skills

General advice

A total of 60 marks are available for Unit 1. Marks will be awarded for demonstrating the following skills:

- focusing on the requirements of the question, for example the topic, the period specified and the 'key concept'
- remembering, choosing and using historical knowledge
- analysing, explaining and reaching a judgement
- showing links between the key factors of your explanation

Focusing on the requirements of the question

Read the question carefully to ensure that you have noted the topic, the period and the 'key concept' that is being addressed. One of the following key concepts will be addressed by each question: causation, consequence, continuity, chance and significance.

In the question 'Why did Stalin emerge as leader of Russia in 1928?' the topic is *the leadership struggle*, the period is *1924–28* and the key concept is causation — *explaining why Stalin won.*

Remembering, choosing and using historical knowledge

When you have established what the question requires, you must decide which aspects of your own knowledge are relevant. You will need between four and six relevant factors: examiners are looking for an answer that covers a wide range of factors. Next you must arrange these factors in a logical order to create a plan for your answer.

Once your structure is in place, you must develop it using specific examples. Try to ensure that your examples are detailed. You should include relevant dates; names of people, places, institutions and events; statistics and appropriate technical vocabulary. Examiners will reward both range and depth of knowledge.

Analysing, explaining and reaching a judgement

Telling the story of an event will not score well. It is expected that your answer will be arranged thematically, addressing different factors in turn.

Your key factors and supporting examples must be explicitly linked back to the question: that is to say, you must show how these details relate to or illustrate the argument that you are making. It is good practice to make these links at the end of each paragraph. It is also important that your essay reaches a clear judgement.

Showing links between the key factors of your explanation

In order to achieve the highest marks, you must highlight links between the factors that you have selected. This could mean demonstrating the relative importance of the different factors, or showing how the factors were dependent on each other.

Level descriptors

Answers are normally marked according to the five levels listed in the table below.

Level	Mark	Descriptor
1	1–6	Candidates produce mostly simple statements. These are supported by limited factual material which has some accuracy and relevance, although not directed at the focus of the question. The material is mostly generalised. There are few, if any, links between the simple statements. The writing may have limited coherence and is generally comprehensible, but passages lack both clarity and organisation. The skills needed to produce effective writing are not normally present. Frequent syntactical and/or spelling errors are likely to be present.
2	7–12	Candidates produce a series of simple statements supported by some mostly accurate and relevant factual material. The analytical focus is mostly implicit and there are likely to be only limited links between the simple statements. Material is unlikely to be developed very far. The writing has some coherence and is generally comprehensible, but passages lack both clarity and organisation. Some of the skills needed to produce effective writing are present. Frequent syntactical and/or spelling errors are likely to be present.
3	13–18	Candidates' answers attempt analysis and show some understanding of the focus of the question. However, they include material that either is descriptive, and thus only implicitly relevant to the question's focus, or which strays from that focus. Factual material will be accurate but it may lack depth and/or relevance in places. The writing is coherent in places but there are likely to be passages that lack clarity and/or proper organisation. Only some of the skills needed to produce convincing extended writing are likely to be present. Syntactical and/or spelling errors are likely to be present.
4	19–24	Candidates offer an analytical response that relates well to the focus of the question and shows some understanding of the key issues contained in it. The analysis is supported by accurate factual material which is mostly relevant to the question asked. The selection of material may lack balance in places. The answer shows some degree of direction and control but these attributes may not be sustained throughout the answer. The candidate demonstrates the skills needed to produce convincing extended writing but there may be passages that lack clarity or coherence. The answer is likely to include some syntactical and/or spelling errors.
5	25–30	Candidates offer an analytical response that directly addresses the focus of the question and demonstrates explicit understanding of the key issues contained in it. It is broadly balanced in its treatment of these key issues. The analysis is supported by accurate, relevant and appropriately selected factual material that demonstrates some range and depth. The exposition is controlled and the deployment logical. Some syntactical and/or spelling errors may be found but the writing is coherent overall. The skills required to produce convincing extended writing are in place.

How to use this guide

First, make sure you understand the layout of the exam paper, the pattern of the marks and the types of question asked, all of which are explained above. Study the outline of the content required, which is given in the Content Guidance section. Try to:

- master the vocabulary and concepts given there
- establish clearly the important individuals and events which shaped the course of these years

The most important part of the guide is the Questions and Answers section, which provides five examples of the kinds of questions that you will be asked. It is important to work through these, studying the two sets of sample answers provided and the examiner's comments. The first answer to each question is an A-grade response that, although not perfect, gives a good idea of what is required. The purpose of the second answer is to illustrate some of the common errors made by students.

Content
Guidance

The specification for **Stalin's Russia, 1924–53** states that the course covers four essential topics:

- The struggle for power — the making of the new *vozhd* 1924–29: personalities and policies.
- Transforming the Soviet Union: the collectivisation of agriculture and its social and economic impact; industrialisation and its economic and social impact; the three Five-Year Plans; changing social policies.
- Persecution and control: the origins and course of the purges; culture and the arts in the service of a totalitarian regime.
- The making of a superpower: the Great Patriotic War; devastation; war production; victory.

This option focuses on the way in which Stalin gained and exercised power between 1924 and 1953. Candidates must be aware of the reasons for Stalin's rise to power as well as his policies once he had gained the supremacy. You need to know how Stalin sought to modernise Russia. This includes his policies that changed agricultural practices, and his Five-Year Plans, which aimed to turn the country into an industrial giant. In addition, you should understand Stalin's aims and policies with regard to the family, women and education in the 1930s.

It is also necessary to be aware of the totalitarian aspect of Stalin's regime. You should know about the causes and events of the Great Terror, including the show trials and wider purges. Furthermore, you should understand how Stalin used art and culture to support his regime. Finally, it is essential to appreciate the USSR's role in the Second World War. Specifically, you should be able to account for its victory and subsequent emergence as a superpower.

This guide considers each of these fundamental topics in turn. However, examiners may set questions which require knowledge from more than one of these areas. For example, a question could be set which requires you to assess the impact of the Great Terror on Stalin's economic policies.

Background

Russia in the early twentieth century

At the beginning of the twentieth century **Russia** was a **feudal society** governed by an emperor, the tsar, who had absolute power. Below the tsar was a rich **aristocracy**. The tsar and the aristocracy owned almost all of Russia's land. At the bottom of Russia's feudal society were the peasants, who comprised approximately 80% of the population. Most of the peasants lived in poverty and did not own the land on which they worked. The money made from the crops they harvested belonged to the landowners. Russia's economy was poorly developed in comparison with those of Western Europe and the USA.

The First World War exposed the fragility of the tsar's government and the backwardness of Russia's economy. The country was unable to produce the weapons and supplies needed for the war or to feed its civilian population. Additionally, Russia's **autocratic** government was unable to organise the war effort effectively, and so Russia lost a great deal of ground. The losses, economic chaos and increased poverty resulting from the war led to unrest among the Russian people and even in the army. In February 1917 riots broke out in Russia's capital city. The tsar ordered the army to stop the protests, but the troops refused to obey orders. Having lost control of the army, the tsar was forced to **abdicate**.

The February Revolution of 1917, which overthrew the tsar, established a new government. The Provisional Government, as it was known, was established as a caretaker administration to manage Russia until a democratic government could be elected. Revolutionary groups such as the **Bolsheviks**, or **Communists** as they became known, began to campaign against the Provisional Government. By September, continuing economic problems and disastrous defeats in the war had made the government deeply unpopular. The Communists were advocating 'Peace, Land and Bread' — an end to the war, redistribution of land to the peasants and economic recovery — and so they grew in popularity. Late in 1917 the Communists, led by Vladimir Ilyich Lenin, organised the October Revolution, an armed uprising in the capital city which overthrew the Provisional Government.

Communist ideology

Lenin and the Communists had a vision for the future of Russia based on the writings of the German philosopher Karl Marx. Lenin believed that history followed a pattern. As a student of Marx, he believed that human society progressed through a series of stages. Marx argued that there was a feudal stage in which society was dominated by kings and aristocrats who oppressed the peasants, which led to a capitalist stage in which the owners of big business oppressed factory workers. After capitalism, Marx believed there would be a period called 'socialism' in which working people governed themselves and worked together for the good of society as a whole. The final stage of human history was called 'communism'. Under communism, there would be no more social classes and everyone would be equal.

Marx claimed that this progress from stage to stage was the result of **class conflict**. In general terms Marx believed that societies were composed of different **classes**, such as the peasants, who worked the land, the working class, who worked in factories, and the middle class or **bourgeoisie**, who owned the factories and the fields in which the other classes worked. These classes were not equal and therefore they fought, and this struggle led to revolutions which were necessary in order to bring about social and political change.

Lenin believed that Russia was entering a stage of history called 'capitalism', in which the bourgeoisie made money by exploiting the **proletariat**, or working class. Again following Marx, Lenin believed that the proletariat would rise up and overthrow the bourgeoisie in a revolution. Lenin hoped that a successful revolution in Russia would establish a socialist government and inspire working-class revolutions first across Europe and then across the globe. These revolutions would end capitalism and exploitation and establish peace, equality and freedom for all working people. Nevertheless, Lenin also argued that there had to be a period known as the 'dictatorship of the proletariat', in which working people, organised by the Communist Party, fought a bitter war against the aristocracy and the bourgeoisie. After all, these people would not give up their positions of power and privilege without a fight.

Russia under Lenin, 1917–21

Lenin's government began with a series of radical and popular **decrees**. The Decree on Land gave the peasants the right to seize land from the aristocratic landowners. The Decree on Peace halted the war with Germany and allowed a peace treaty to be negotiated. The Decree on Workers' Control allowed working people to take over the factories where they worked. These decrees were very popular and won the new government considerable support. However, this support was short-lived. Economic problems continued, and the Treaty of Brest-Litovsk, which ended Russia's involvement in the First World War, led to the loss of a great deal of Russian money and territory. Finally, Lenin refused to establish the kind of democracy that people had hoped for prior to the Communist revolution. Instead, he set up a government entirely consisting of Communists. He also closed down the new democratically elected government that he had promised prior to the October Revolution.

As a result of the continuing economic problems, the humiliating treaty and the broken promise of a democratically elected government, Lenin's government faced considerable opposition. By early summer 1918 a civil war had broken out between the Communist Reds and the opposing Whites, a collection of armed factions wanting either a return to tsarism, a restoration of democracy or an alternative form of socialism.

During the Civil War of 1918–21 Lenin's government took a series of unpopular measures in order to ensure victory. War Communism, the economic policy of the government during the war, was particularly resented. War Communism included the following measures:

- The requisitioning of grain from Russia's peasants. Essentially, the peasants were expected to work without making a profit. Consequently, agricultural production fell dramatically.
- Government control of industry, which ended workers' control.
- The abolition of money and the imposition of rationing.

The army was also reorganised. The Provisional Government had abolished the death penalty, but Leon Trotsky, Communist leader of the **Red Army**, reintroduced the death penalty to ensure that there was strict discipline among his soldiers.

War Communism and army reform were deeply unpopular with Russia's workers and peasants. The Communists survived, however, because they used ruthless repression against their enemies. Freedom of the press was abolished and elections postponed, and the Communist secret police used torture and murder to eliminate their political enemies.

Lenin and the NEP

By early 1921 the Communists had won the military victory, but the country had been ruined. The Communists' economic policies had led to a famine. In order to revive the economy Lenin introduced the New Economic Policy (NEP). This ended the rationing and requisitioning of War Communism, replacing them with a limited form of capitalism. The NEP allowed peasants to sell their produce and make a profit, while the government taxed them and invested the money in industry. To many Communists, the NEP was a betrayal of the ideas for which they had fought in the Civil War, but the Russian economy had collapsed, and the majority supported the NEP as a temporary measure to help rebuild it.

This economic reform was not matched by political reform. Lenin's regime refused to allow a democratic form of government. Indeed, in 1921 the Communists outlawed the few opposition parties that had survived the Civil War. Additionally, the Communists retained control of the press. Finally, Lenin decided that discipline within the Communist Party needed to be tightened. Following the Civil War the party had split into several **factions** which opposed Lenin's policies. He dealt with this by imposing a ban on factions. The ban on opposition political parties closed down debate outside the party, while the ban on factions ended debate within the party itself.

Lenin's death

In mid-1922 Lenin had the first of a series of strokes. At first he made a good recovery, and returned to work in the autumn of 1922. However, at the end of that year he had another stroke. Though confined to bed, he continued to monitor the government and to influence its decisions by writing letters to key ministers. In early 1923, fearing the worst, Lenin wrote his last letters to the party, discussing the strengths and weaknesses of the leading figures who would govern Russia once he was dead. By the end of January 1923 he had suffered yet another stroke, leaving him unable to speak. Lenin lived for another year, but he was unable to communicate and therefore could take no further part in government.

Glossary

abdicate: to give up power.

aristocracy: the nobility.

autocratic: a system in which a ruler exercises absolute power.

Bolsheviks: the original name of the Communist Party in Russia.

bourgeoisie: a technical term used by Marxists to describe the middle class.

class conflict: struggles between social classes that result from one class oppressing the other.

classes: social groups which are different from one another on account of their economic position and role.

Communists: the name adopted by the Bolshevik Party in 1918.

decrees: laws.

factions: small groups within a political party.

feudal society: a hierarchical society in which the king rules, aided by the nobility.

proletariat: a technical term used by Marxists to describe the working class.

Red Army: the army of the Communists.

Russia: before February 1917, Russia was officially known as the Russian Empire. In 1922, the Communist government in Russia united with neighbouring regions to form the Union of Soviet Socialist Republics (USSR or Soviet Union).

The leadership struggle

The nature of the leadership struggle

When Lenin died in January 1924, the leadership struggle was already underway. Early in 1923 leading Communists recognised that Lenin would never recover, and they began competing for control of the party and government.

It is important to remember that Russia — by this time part of the Soviet Union — was not a democracy, and therefore the leadership struggle was not about winning popularity with the people. The struggle for power was fought inside the Communist Party, and therefore influence within the party was important. Lenin's authority was not based on any of his official positions. Rather, Lenin was the leader of the party because the party ranks respected him and because he could count on the loyalty of the most important members of the government. In order to become the next ruler, one of the contenders would have to command the same level of respect, and so they all began stressing their similarities to Lenin. All the contenders claimed to be Lenin's most loyal follower, and all argued that they understood his ideas, or Leninism as it became know, better than anyone else.

The contenders

Five main contenders for power emerged in 1923. The most obvious person to lead the country was Leon Trotsky. He was well known for his heroism during the revolution and the Civil War. He had organised the October Revolution and successfully commanded the Red Army during its war with the Whites. From 1917 to 1922 he had been Lenin's right-hand man. Trotsky was also a charismatic speaker and an intellectual. His radicalism, his strong personality and his heroic history made him very attractive to the students and young people in the party. He also enjoyed the respect of the Red Army. Nevertheless, he was not universally supported. Trotsky had joined the party in mid 1917, and so some who had party members for many years resented his success and claimed he was not a proper Communist. Moreover, many feared his radical ideas. Russia had experienced a period of continuous war and revolution from 1914 to 1921 and was in a state of ruin. **Pragmatists** within the party believed that Trotsky's radical ideas would lead to further ruin, and so favoured moderate policies and a period of stability rather than the prospect of more radical adventures under him.

Zinoviev and Kamenev, who had been Lenin's closest friends, believed that they should lead the party. They enjoyed some respect as long-standing Communists and close comrades of Lenin. They were also known for being moderate and so enjoyed the support of pragmatists in the party. However, Trotsky argued that they were too cautious. Immediately prior to the October Revolution Zinoviev and Kamenev had criticised Lenin for planning to overthrow the Provisional Government. Trotsky argued that at this crucial moment they had been cowards and disloyal to Lenin. Zinoviev and Kamenev had also been criticised during the Civil War for staying well away from the fighting and using their power to ensure that they lived in luxury.

The youngest contender for leadership was Bukharin. He had fought bravely in the revolutionary period of late 1917 and had made an important contribution to the Communist victory in the Civil War through managing the press and organising Communist **propaganda**. Bukharin's friendly and honest personality also made him very popular within the party. Lenin had publicly shown his faith in Bukharin by naming him the party's chief **theorist**. At the same time, it was well known that he had disagreed with Lenin on theoretical issues in 1916, which indicated to some that he was not a true Leninist. Some also argued that he was simply too young to take over the leadership of the party and the country. Finally, from 1921 Bukharin had supported the NEP with great vigour. This made him unpopular with radicals within the party who saw his enthusiasm for the capitalist NEP as a betrayal of communism.

In 1923 Stalin seemed the least likely candidate to succeed Lenin as leader of the party. He had fulfilled an important administrative function during the Civil War, but his role was much less public and glamorous than that of Trotsky or Bukharin. He was not an outstanding speaker or intellectual, and could not compete with Trotsky or Bukharin in these areas. However, Stalin was seen by many as the safe candidate. Trotsky represented the extreme **left wing** of the party and Bukharin represented its **right wing**. Many Communists regarded both wings of the party with suspicion, and saw Trotsky and Bukharin as too intellectual. Stalin, by contrast, was a **centrist**, and could therefore present himself as a sensible and practical politician.

The issues

The struggle for power was fought out through two protracted debates about the country's future: in particular, its economic policy and its role in the world. In general terms, the party's left wing held one position on these issues and the right wing held another. Notably, some of the contenders switched sides during the debate.

Economic

In terms of economic policy the right wing was committed to the NEP. Bukharin, the leading figure on the right, argued that the NEP was leading to economic growth and was therefore working well. Within a year the NEP had solved the problem of the famine, and by 1926 industry was also recovering. Moreover, Bukharin argued that Lenin had been committed to the NEP and had wanted Russia to maintain the policy for many years.

The left wing, headed by Trotsky, disagreed. Trotsky argued that the NEP was a short-term policy that had outlived its usefulness. He claimed that the NEP was dangerous because it was partially capitalist and therefore allowed some peasants and traders to grow rich while others remained poor. This kind of inequality was a feature of capitalism, and the Communists had a duty to stamp it out. Trotsky's alternative was a policy similar to War Communism: the government should organise the economy and use the wealth generated by the peasants to invest in industry. It should encourage small farms to join together into **collective farms**, and should use its power and resources to plan rapid industrialisation.

Initially, the left-wing policies were unpopular because they risked starting another civil war. The peasants, who were the majority of the population, hated War Communism and supported the NEP. Knowing that the peasants would oppose government control of farms, the majority in the party supported the NEP, which had led to economic growth and peace.

Russia and the world

The Communists were also divided on their position in the world. The left wing argued that communism in Russia could never be secure as long as the rest of the world was capitalist. Hostile capitalist governments in Europe and the USA could gang up on Russia, invade and overthrow the government. Trotsky therefore advocated a policy known as 'permanent revolution', whereby the government would send aid to foreign Communist parties in order to inspire revolutions throughout Europe and the rest of the world.

The party's right, on the other hand, advocated the policy of 'socialism in one country'. According to Bukharin and Stalin, socialism could develop in Russia alone as long as the government stayed strong and cracked down on opposition within the country.

'Socialism in one country' proved much more attractive to the Communist Party. First, it appealed to nationalism because it suggested that Russia had a special status in the world and that its people could achieve great things without relying on the rest of the world. Second, 'permanent revolution' implied continuing conflict with other countries, and many Communists wanted to avoid war so that Russia could repair the damage it had sustained during the First World War and the Civil War. Finally, Trotsky's idea of permanent revolution appeared to be very **defeatist** because it implied that the Russian Revolution was doomed to fail unless the rest of the world also had a revolution.

Institutional factors

Stalin's position within Soviet institutions gave him a great advantage over his rivals for power. Unlike them, he wielded enormous influence over the lower ranks of the party. In 1922 he had been appointed General Secretary of the Communist Party. This gave him extensive powers of **patronage**: he was responsible for appointing people to key positions within the party and for promotions. As head of the Workers' and Peasants' Inspectorate and the Central Control Commission, he also had the power to sack party members. This position of patronage won Stalin the loyalty of the junior ranks of the party who were keen for promotion and the higher wages and status it entailed. Second, as General Secretary, Stalin was able to manipulate the system which decided who attended the **Party Congresses**. As time went by, an increasing number of delegates to these were effectively appointed by Stalin. This in turn gave Stalin a powerful influence on the composition of the party's **Central Committee**, as this was selected by junior party members through the Congress. Finally, Stalin was also responsible for recruitment. In 1921, roughly one-quarter of the Communist Party's members were serving in the Red Army and were therefore loyal to Trotsky. However, the recruitment drive known as the **Lenin Enrolment** in 1923–25 enabled Stalin to increase the size of the party and thereby reduce Trotsky's influence.

Stalin's opponents had important-sounding job titles, but little real institutional power. Trotsky, as leader of the Red Army, could do nothing without the sanction of the **Politburo**. Zinoviev and Kamenev's power was concentrated in the local parties in Moscow and **Petrograd**. While these were significant positions, support in Moscow and Petrograd was little help at the Party Congress, as the Congress represented the whole country. Bukharin's control of the media and education was a potential threat to Stalin, but Stalin was able to use his organisational power to appoint Bukharin's deputies and thus restrict his ability to use the media effectively. Zinoviev and Bukharin also had senior positions in the **Comintern**. These were prestigious but lacked power, because the Comintern had no governmental role.

Lenin's legacy

Stalin's power was in many ways a product of the party and governmental system created by Lenin. In order to win power, Stalin capitalised on the structure of the party and the ideology that Lenin had created, while suppressing Lenin's final attempt to guide the future of Russia.

Between 1917 and 1922, Lenin had created a highly authoritarian and centralised system of government which Stalin was able to manipulate to remove his rivals. The abolition of democracy and rival political parties ensured that the next ruler of Russia would be a member of the Communist Party. Lenin's abolition of civil rights outlawed opposition to the Communist Party. At the same time, Lenin had also curtailed the rights of those within the Communist Party — the 1921 Ban on Factions prevented minority groups within the party from challenging the power of the party leadership. Stalin used this system to reprimand first Trotsky, then Zinoviev and Kamenev, and finally Bukharin for factional activity. Lenin had also created a highly bureaucratic party. Stalin was a gifted administrator and so was able to manipulate the party to achieve his own ends. He was able to control the flow of information, the hiring and firing of party officials and the implementation of policy through his position as General Secretary, which, as Lenin had noted, concentrated unlimited power in his hands.

Lenin had continually stressed the importance of pursuing the correct ideological goals. At the same time, his writings were often unclear and contradictory. Stalin echoed Lenin's call for ideological purity and criticised his opponents for diverging from Leninism. However, he also capitalised on Lenin's ambiguity in order to justify his doctrine of 'socialism in one country' and his final break with the NEP.

Although Stalin did not create the Cult of Lenin, he soon became its high priest and the guardian of Lenin's memory. Stalin's religious training had made him aware of the power of religious imagery as well as the doctrines of the Orthodox Church. He manipulated the feelings of new members of the Communist Party by combining devotion to Lenin with traditional religious symbolism. Stalin's speech at Lenin's funeral is a good example of the way in which he used religious language to present himself as a true Leninist.

Alliances and tactics

In order to exercise power it was essential to command a majority in the Politburo. Lenin had dominated the Politburo, but none of his would-be successors was held in the same respect by its members. The contenders for power therefore had to make alliances in order to gain control of the Politburo.

The Triumvirate vs the Left Opposition, 1923–25

When it became obvious that Lenin was not going to recover from his illness, Zinoviev and Kamenev acted quickly to prevent Trotsky becoming the leader. Together with Stalin they formed a triumvirate, or three-person alliance, which gave them a majority against Trotsky in the Politburo. In return for his support, Stalin asked Zinoviev and Kamenev to help him to deal with Lenin's *Testament*, a document in which Lenin spelled out the strengths and weaknesses of the contenders for power. The *Testament* had the potential to be highly damaging for Stalin. Lenin argued that Stalin had gained too much power in his position as General Secretary and that he was too rude to use this power wisely. Lenin asked party leaders to dismiss Stalin and replace him with a more trustworthy figure. If Stalin were sacked it would mean the end of his political career. Zinoviev and Kamenev supported Stalin and argued that he had learned his lesson and therefore should retain his post. They also argued that Lenin's *Testament*, which criticised every one of the contenders, should be kept secret as it would damage the authority of the government. The Central Committee agreed with their argument: Stalin kept his job and the *Testament* was kept secret.

The Triumvirate's main purpose was to keep Trotsky, and his Left Opposition supporters, out of power. They used a dirty tricks campaign against Trotsky to achieve this. First, Stalin, who organised Lenin's funeral, told Trotsky the wrong date for the ceremony. As a result Trotsky, who was away from Moscow at the time, missed it. The Triumvirate then claimed that Trotsky's absence was a sign of disrespect for Lenin. Moreover, Stalin was able to use the opportunity to make a declaration of his loyalty to Lenin in front of the most important members of the party who had gathered to mourn their leader. Second, Zinoviev and Kamenev published histories of the revolution and the Civil War which implied that Trotsky had not played a very big role in these events. Finally, Stalin used his power as General Secretary to initiate the Lenin Enrolment. This greatly increased the size of the party, filling it with new members who had no memory of Trotsky's heroism in the Civil War. Moreover, the new members were poorly educated and so did not understand Trotsky's complex ideas. The campaign against Trotsky was highly successful, and in 1925 the economic policies of Trotsky and the Left Opposition were rejected by the Party Congress.

The Duumvirate, 1925–27

The Triumvirate was united in opposition to Trotsky, but after defeating him at the 1925 Party Congress they no longer had a reason to work together. Stalin and Bukharin began collaborating in their shared commitment to the doctrine of socialism in one country, but Zinoviev and Kamenev rejected the idea.

Following the breakdown of the Triumvirate, the Duumvirate of Bukharin and Stalin, supported by Bukharin's allies Rykov and Tomsky, swiftly emerged as the ruling coalition in the Politburo. These four members made up the majority in the Politburo, while Zinoviev, Kamenev and Trotsky formed the minority. Between 1925 and 1926 Zinoviev and Kamenev opposed Bukharin and Stalin over the extent to which socialism could be built in one country only. Zinoviev and Kamenev argued that Lenin had always championed a world revolution, while Bukharin and Stalin argued that the doctrine of world revolution was defeatist and unpatriotic.

In 1926, Zinoviev and Kamenev formed an alliance with Trotsky, calling themselves the United Opposition. This required Zinoviev and Kamenev to shift positions on the NEP and to embrace the left-wing vision of rapid industrialisation and agricultural collectivisation. Importantly, many in the party were not convinced by the United Opposition. Zinoviev and Kamenev had spent 1923 and 1925 campaigning against Trotsky, and therefore their alliance looked like a tactical move to gain power. Once again, the Duumvirate won against the opposition. The Duumvirate's success was due to Bukharin's excellent public speaking at the 1927 Congress and Stalin's ability to pack the Congress with his supporters. Following the Duumvirate's victory Zinoviev, Kamenev and Trotsky were sacked from the Politburo and expelled from the party. Zinoviev and Kamenev apologised and were allowed to rejoin the party, but Trotsky refused and was exiled from Russia.

Stalin versus Bukharin, 1928–29

Three new members were elected to the Politburo to replace Zinoviev, Kamenev and Trotsky. All three supported Stalin. Stalin now had a majority and no longer needed the support of Bukharin and his allies Rykov and Tomsky. Stalin used his new strength to make a bold move: he rejected the NEP and endorsed the left-wing economic policy of rapid industrialisation and agricultural collectivisation. His position thus became very attractive: he still advocated socialism in one country and therefore appealed to Russian nationalism, but he also now appealed to the left wing, who had lost their leaders when Zinoviev, Kamenev and Trotsky were defeated and humiliated. Moreover, Stalin's move away from the NEP came at the perfect time. During 1927 the NEP began experiencing new problems. The Russian peasants started producing less grain in order to force its price up. This problem continued into 1928, and pragmatists who had supported the NEP because it was working started to question the policy and look for alternatives.

Stalin's first move against the NEP was to send government agents into the countryside to take grain by force from the peasants, causing outbreaks of conflict and violence. Bukharin used his power to stop the policy, and Stalin backed down. However, this retreat was only temporary, and by mid-1928 Stalin had ordered forced collectivisation of agriculture. Bukharin and his allies fought this policy, but Stalin had used his position as General Secretary to appoint his supporters to important posts and they were able to block Bukharin's efforts. In an attempt to defeat Stalin, Bukharin had a secret meeting with Zinoviev and Kamenev, but Stalin's agents found out about it and accused Bukharin, Zinoviev and Kamenev of breaking Lenin's ban on factions. Stalin also used his influence to stop Bukharin attending important meetings. In one case, when Bukharin was flying back to a meeting in Moscow, Stalin ordered that his plane be grounded and that Bukharin submit to medical examinations before being allowed to continue his flight.

Victory

By the end of 1928 Bukharin had lost the fight. Stalin had shown that he had a majority of support in the Central Committee and the Politburo, and so was able to continue his policy of collectivisation and launch his new industrial policy, the First Five-Year Plan. Bukharin and his allies remained in the Politburo but were unable to block Stalin's policies. By the end of the year Bukharin was expelled from the Politburo.

Conclusion

By 1928, Stalin was recognised as Russia's **vozhd**. His victory was a combination of personal, institutional, historical, ideological and tactical factors. His lack of distinction was actually one of his greatest strengths, because his mediocrity threatened no one. At the same time, his understanding of the mindset of the new party recruits allowed him to appeal to their interests in a way that the more Western members of the party leadership could not. Equally, loyalty to Stalin offered great rewards, while disloyalty could be sternly punished. Unlike his opponents, Stalin had never had a public disagreement with Lenin. In addition, Stalin was ideally suited to manipulating the bureaucratic and authoritarian party machine that Lenin had created. Ideologically, Stalin offered a simple, optimistic vision that directly appealed to Russian nationalism. Finally, Stalin was a devious tactician who was superficially loyal to his colleagues while at the same time plotting their downfall.

Stalin was an unlikely heir to Lenin. Zinoviev and Kamenev had been Lenin's best friends and closest collaborators, Trotsky was the best known of Lenin's lieutenants, and Bukharin was the 'favourite of the whole party' as well as its official theorist. But it was Stalin who thrived in the bureaucratic and treacherous environment that Lenin had left behind, and therefore it was Stalin who won the right to impose his vision of socialism on the USSR.

Glossary

Central Committee: a group of Communists elected by the Party Congress to manage party affairs between meetings of the Congress.

centrist: a person or organisation adopting a political position between the left and right wings.

collective farms: farms owned by the state, on which productive resources were shared.

Comintern: the Communist International, an institution tasked with spreading Communist revolution across the globe.

defeatist: giving up easily.

left wing: in this context, the wing of the Communist Party that was committed to radical measures such as the collectivisation of agriculture and rapid industrialisation.

Lenin Enrolment: a drive in 1923–25 to recruit more workers as members of the Communist Party.

Party Congress: a meeting of delegates representing the entire Communist Party, held annually until 1926, then less frequently.

patronage: the power to make appointments to government jobs, especially for political advantage.

Petrograd: a city in northwest Russia, known as Leningrad from 1924 to 1991, now called St Petersburg.

Politburo: the highest committee within the Communist Party — effectively Russia's governing council from October 1917.

pragmatist: someone who takes a practical, rather than ideological, approach to politics.

propaganda: publicity material designed to promote a certain point of view.

right wing: in this context, the wing of the Communist Party that was committed to moderate measures such as the NEP.

theorist: an intellectual who devotes his/her time to considering ideological questions.

vozhd: a Russian word meaning 'leader' and used to refer to Stalin. Unlike, say, 'prime minister' or 'president', it does not denote a specific official post, and so implies unlimited and general power.

The economy in the 1930s

Stalin's economic policies in agriculture and industry were based on his Marxist ideology. Marxists wanted to replace free-market capitalism with a planned economic system, on the grounds that a **free market** allows some people to become rich while others remain poor. They believed that a planned economy could create a system where everyone was equal.

The collectivisation of agriculture

Collectivisation was the process by which Soviet agriculture was reformed. Traditional, small peasant farms were replaced by large-scale farms owned by the government. In theory this would lead to greater efficiency, as peasants could share resources and work together. However, the majority of peasants protested against collectivisation because they were no longer allowed to own their land.

The reasons for collectivisation

Stalin decided to collectivise for a range of economic, ideological and political reasons. First, after 1926 there was a grain procurement crisis: in 1926, the country's farmers produced 77 million tonnes of grain, but by 1927 this had fallen to 72 million tonnes. Second, the government's plan to industrialise relied on profits gained by selling grain abroad. The fall in grain production meant that the government was unable to meet its industrialisation targets in 1927 and 1928. Third, many Communist Party members were ideologically opposed to the capitalist elements in the NEP and wanted in the long term to replace it with a more socialist system. Fourth, by introducing collectivisation Stalin demonstrated that he, rather than Bukharin, was in control of Russia. Finally, Stalin knew very little about agriculture or Russian peasants and their farming methods, and this led him to adopt unrealistic policies, including collectivisation.

Collectivisation in action

Stalin introduced collectivisation in stages, introducing radical policies only to backtrack later. First, in the winter of 1928–29, he brought in emergency measures to deal with the grain procurement crisis. He criminalised the hoarding of grain and introduced rationing of bread and sugar in the cities. He also gave the police powers to round up so-called '**kulaks**' who interfered with or held back the production of grain.

Stalin's second step towards collectivisation was the 'liquidation of the kulaks as a class'. This policy, which was also known as 'de-kulakisation', marked the beginning of an official war on capitalism in the countryside. Members of the Red Army, the secret police and the Communist Party were sent into villages to look for grain and to force peasants to join collective farms. Those who resisted were labelled kulaks and deported to labour camps in Siberia or killed, and their property was redistributed to newly established collective farms. The kulaks, however, fought back and refused to surrender their resources to the state farms. Around 18 million horses and 100 million sheep and goats were destroyed by kulaks between 1929 and 1933.

His third step was to call off the policy of de-kulakisation and collectivisation because of the havoc it was creating in the countryside. In March 1930, Stalin published an article in **Pravda** entitled 'Dizzy with Success'. He blamed the problems created by his collectivisation campaign on local party members who had been 'over-enthusiastic'. At the time the article was published, approximately 50% of Russia's farms had been collectivised. However, following Stalin's policy reversal, the number of collective farms dropped, and by August 1930 only a quarter of the country's farms remained collective.

The consequences of collectivisation

Collectivisation had economic, social and political consequences. In terms of economics, collectivisation led to a famine between 1932 and 1934. Many peasants had destroyed their livestock, crops and machinery rather than give them to collective farms, and production fell as a result. Additionally, the total labour force working on Russia's farms dropped. As many as 10 million peasants were exiled between 1929 and 1931 as part of the collectivisation process. In some areas 10% of the peasants were exiled. Again, this reduction in the labour force resulted in a fall in production. Nonetheless, Stalin was determined to export grain in order to raise money for his industrialisation plans. This combination of decreased production and increased exports led to an unprecedented famine in which approximately 10 million people died.

In terms of social consequences, Stalin's collectivisation policy played a part in increasing the proportion of the Russian population who lived in cities. In 1928, approximately 18% of Soviet citizens were urban. By 1939, this figure had risen to 50%. The trend towards urbanisation began in the early 1930s as peasants fled the countryside in order to escape the famine.

Finally, collectivisation also had political consequences. The famine in the countryside and the scarcity of food in the cities created a feeling of crisis at the top of the Communist Party. Stalin exploited this to demand greater loyalty, and many Communists stood behind him, fearing that the opponents of communism would use the crisis to start a civil war. Additionally, the famine can be seen as a deliberate policy against the peasants, as Stalin's government prioritised grain exports over feeding their own people. Indeed, in areas such as the **Ukraine** Stalin deliberately cancelled grain deliveries during the famine in order to show rebellious peasants that his regime would not tolerate opposition. In this way, the failure of Stalin's policy strengthened his position and further consolidated his power.

The First Five-Year Plan (1928–32)

The origins of the planned economy

The Five-Year Plans were designed to replace capitalism with a more organised and fairer economic system, to industrialise the USSR's economy so that it would catch up and overtake those of capitalist countries, and finally, to show that Stalin was a visionary who deserved to be the leader.

Ideologically, Stalin, along with all Marxists, believed that socialism was only possible in an advanced industrial nation. The Soviet Union, however, was a peasant country, and so Stalin was convinced that socialism was impossible without enormous economic growth. The Communists also believed that the proletariat was the revolutionary class that would build socialism. In this sense, the Five-Year Plan was necessary, because it would increase the number of working-class people in Russia by encouraging peasants to leave the countryside and work in the factories. Finally, a planned economy had been a long-standing vision of Communists on the left wing of the party, and the ideological debates during the leadership struggle of the 1920s set out the reasons why a planned economy was preferable to capitalism and the NEP.

The Five-Year Plan was also introduced for economic reasons. First, it was designed to industrialise Russia at the fastest possible pace: Stalin hoped to catch up with countries such as the USA and Britain in the space of 10 years. He believed that growth of this kind was only possible if the government gained total control of the economy. The NEP's failure to industrialise Russia had persuaded many Communists that a greater degree of planning and government intervention was necessary to achieve this. Stalin believed that the radical transformation of agriculture through collectivisation meant industry too could be revolutionised. Moreover, he hoped, by making farming more efficient, collectivisation would release labour and resources for his industrial plans.

Politically, the Five-Year Plans were designed to show that Stalin had an ambitious vision for Russia. In this sense the launch of the First Five-Year Plan was a symbolic shift from Lenin's Russia, the Russia of the NEP, to Stalin's Russia. The Five-Year Plan also demonstrated Stalin's victory over Bukharin, who was the leading advocate of the NEP. Finally, Stalin's advocacy of the Five-Year Plan allowed him to gain the support of the left wing of the party, which had been leaderless since the expulsion of Trotsky in 1927. In this way the adoption of the First Five-Year Plan was a continuation of the leadership struggle, since it showed that Stalin was able to implement his own policies and, in so doing, consolidate his position.

The nature and priorities of the Plan

The Five-Year Plans were based on a series of production targets drawn up by **Gosplan**. Essentially, Gosplan set targets for every factory, workshop, mine and mill in Russia. The targets were extremely ambitious, and Stalin hoped that if they were all met or exceeded the economy would grow. Notably, little thought was given to the needs of the people who would use the products manufactured by the Plan, so there was a lack of quality control and little focus on **consumer goods**. The Plan also made use of prison labour. Approximately 10 million people were sent to **gulags** as part of the campaign against the kulaks, and many were used as slave labour on the projects of the Five-Year Plan. For example, 40,000 prison workers were set to work on building the new city of Magnitogorsk, on the edge of Siberia.

The priority of the First Five-Year Plan was the growth of heavy industry. Stalin was aiming for a huge increase in production of coal, oil, iron and steel. He believed that heavy industry was 'the basic, decisive branch of industry', because historically, in Europe and the USA, heavy industry was the first branch of industry to grow. Stalin assumed that Russia would follow the same pattern. Additionally, he believed that consumer goods were a feature of capitalism and that a socialist society should emphasise hard work rather than luxuries and an easy life.

How successful was the Plan?

In terms of production growth in heavy industry, the Plan was an undoubted success. The production of iron, steel, coal and oil all rose. For example, iron production increased from 3.3 million tonnes in 1928 to 6.2 million tonnes in 1932. Similarly, steel production increased from 4.0 million tonnes in 1929 to 5.9 million tonnes in 1932. Coal production increased from 35.4 million tonnes to 64.3 million tonnes in the same period, and oil production from 11.7 million tonnes in 1928 to 21.4 million tonnes in 1932. In all of these areas, the targets for the Plan were 'overfulfilled'. During the First Five-Year Plan, the Russian economy as a whole grew by 14% per year, and Stalin claimed that the Plan was highly successful.

The Plan also had a big impact on **social mobility**. The urban population increased threefold as peasants moved to the cities to find work in industry. Members of the working class were promoted, often becoming industrial managers or '**red specialists**'.

Nevertheless, there were difficulties with the Plan. First, many of the targets were never actually met: local administrators and party officials lied about the scale of production in order to impress the party leaders and avoid being sacked or sent to prison camps. For example, the target for iron production was 8 million tonnes: Stalin claimed that this target was met, but it is now believed that the total amount of iron produced by 1932 was only 6.2 million tonnes. Equally, because the focus of the Plan was on the quantity of production, there was little concern about the quality. Consequently, some of the iron and steel produced was of such low quality that it was useless. Finally, because the focus of the Plan was on production rather than consumption, much of what was produced was never used.

Living standards did not improve during the First Five-Year Plan, because this was not one of the priorities of the Plan. The rationing introduced in the last years of the NEP continued throughout the First Five-Year Plan, and the diet of Soviet workers was poorer than it had been under the NEP. Additionally, working conditions were harsh: for example, Stalin introduced a 7-day working week and workers lost their traditional day off on Sundays. Many factories were hastily constructed and consequently unsafe.

The Second Five-Year Plan (1933–37)

The priorities of the Plan

The priorities of the Second Five-Year Plan were significantly different to those of the First. Initially, the Second Five-Year Plan explicitly emphasised improvement of living standards as a target. However, in 1936 there was a shift in priorities, and resources that had been devoted to creating consumer goods were redirected towards heavy industry and rearmament. The Second Five-Year Plan also stressed the improvement of communications, roads, railways and canals, as well as developing more specialist areas of the economy, such as chemical industries. Finally, the Second Five-Year Plan aimed to increase the production of electricity. Overall, the aim of the Second Five-Year Plan was to modernise Soviet industry.

The priorities changed for a number of reasons. First, Soviet planners learned from the experience of the First Five-Year Plan and decided it was necessary to develop the economy in a more rounded way. The focus on communications was based on a recognition that although the First Five-Year Plan had successfully produced a lot of raw materials, it was still difficult to move these products around the country. The planners also devised methods to increase **labour productivity**, recognising that although Soviet citizens worked long hours, they produced less per hour than workers in Western countries. To combat this, they introduced incentives to boost labour productivity. Second, moderates in the Politburo, led by Sergei Kirov, argued that Soviet citizens needed to benefit from economic growth. They put pressure on Stalin to modify the Plan and devote more resources to consumer goods. However, following Kirov's murder at the end of 1934, Politburo moderates lost their influence and Stalin was able to redirect resources to heavy industry. Finally, the growing might of Nazi Germany forced a change of course, and the second half of the Plan emphasised rearmament in anticipation of war with Germany.

How successful was the Plan?

Initially, the Second Five-Year Plan was very successful, particularly in terms of improving the living standards of Soviet workers. Between 1934 and 1936 the people enjoyed 'three good years' during which rationing of products such as bread and meat ended. After 1936, however, living standards declined as resources were diverted to heavy industry and rearmament.

Labour productivity certainly increased in the first years of the Second Five-Year Plan. Alexei Stakhanov became the model for all Soviet workers. Stakhanov, a miner in the Donets Basin coal region, was reported to have mined 227 tonnes of coal in a single shift. This was more than 20 times the amount of coal produced by the average Soviet miner. He was rewarded with 200 roubles (the equivalent of 1 month's wages), a new apartment with a telephone, and cinema tickets. These rewards were extended to all workers who exceeded their targets, and helped bring about a rise in labour productivity.

In heavy industry, production increased. For example, the output of steel tripled during the Second Five-Year Plan. Transport also improved. For example, the Moscow metro was opened in 1935, improving transport within Russia's capital, and the Moscow–Volga Canal, completed in 1937, facilitated the transportation of raw materials throughout western Russia. Finally, defence spending rose from 4% of government expenditure in 1933 to 17% in 1937.

But there were problems with the Plan. Even during the 'three good years' there were shortages of essential goods such as shoes. In 1934, 6,000 people queued for more than a day outside a shoe shop after hearing a rumour that there would soon be a delivery of shoes. Equally, from 1936 the administration of the Plan deteriorated, because many managers and planners were imprisoned or executed as part of Stalin's Great Terror.

The Third Five-Year Plan (1938–41)

The priorities of the Plan

The Third Five-Year Plan had two priorities: heavy industry and rearmament. These were related, as heavy industry provided the raw materials for military hardware. Once again, the planners gave little priority to living standards and consumer goods. These priorities reflected the growing concern that Russia would soon be at war with Germany (the Plan only ran until 1941 when Russia entered the Second World War). They also showed that Stalin's Terror had successfully removed party moderates who had argued for greater focus on consumer goods.

How successful was the Plan?

The Third Five-Year Plan successfully diverted economic resources to rearmament. By 1940, a third of all investment went to the armed forces, and during the Plan military spending more than doubled. Production of heavy industry also increased. The production of coal, for example, went up from 128 million tonnes in 1937 to 166 million tonnes in 1940. However, crude oil and steel production stagnated.

The Third Five-Year Plan was poorly administered. Stalin's purges created chaos in Gosplan and removed many factory managers, with the result that the Plan lacked both central direction and competent local management. The country saw a return to the chaotic administration that had characterised the First Five-Year Plan.

Conclusion

The first three Five-Year Plans led to a huge increase in industrial production. This was achieved, however, at the expense of living standards. Soviet planners had a one-sided view of the Russian economy, continually emphasising heavy industry at the expense of consumer goods. With the exception of the 'three good years', the economic growth did not benefit the Soviet people.

The growth in industry was not matched in agriculture. Grain production in the 1930s was consistently lower than it had been in the 1920s. The system of collective farms failed to motivate farmers to produce. For this reason, agriculture recovered slowly from the famine of 1932–34.

Glossary

consumer goods: products that are designed to satisfy people's needs and desires.
free market: an economic system in which goods and services are traded with minimal government intervention.
Gosplan: the government department responsible for drawing up, implementing and monitoring economic plans.
gulags: prison camps.
kulaks: rich peasants.
labour productivity: the measure of how productive people are when working.
Pravda: Communist newspaper.
red specialists: industrial experts who originated from the working class and were promoted to replace 'bourgeois specialists' during Stalin's First Five-Year Plan.
social mobility: movement between different social groups.
Ukraine: a republic in the west of the USSR known for its agricultural production. Since 1991, Ukraine has been an independent state.

Stalin's social policies

Objectives

Stalin's aims for social policy tied in with his broader aims for the economy. In general terms, he wanted women, the family and education to serve the needs of collective farming and the Five-Year Plans. Social policy therefore emphasised discipline, hard work and respect for authority.

Stalin's social policy was a marked contrast to the one pursued by the Communists in the 1920s. In that decade, Communist policy emphasised women's freedom, particularly their rights to divorce, state-provided childcare and abortion on demand. It also emphasised sexual freedom: homosexuality was legalised, and some leading Communists experimented with '**free love**'. In schools, the Communists emphasised equality between students and teachers and a revolutionary syllabus that encouraged Communist ideals. Stalinist policy was much more traditional: Trotsky named it 'the Great Retreat'.

Women

Stalin's social policy encouraged women to join the workforce in large numbers. In 1928, only 3 million women were employed in industry, whereas by 1940 the number was 13 million. The government also increased the number of places in higher and technical education available to women, from 20% in 1929 to 40% in 1940. Women's pay, however, was only approximately 65% that of men. Women workers were also important in agriculture: by 1945, with many men fighting in the war, approximately 80% of collective farm workers were women. Indeed, Russia's most famous agricultural Stakhanovites — Pasha Angelina and Maria Demchenko — were women. Demchenko, for example, pledged to harvest four times the average yield of sugar beet and was rewarded highly when she fulfilled her pledge.

Women were also expected to bear and raise the next generation, and the Communist government introduced incentives for them to have large families. Any woman who had more than six children would receive state help. Mothers of seven children received 2,000 roubles a year for 5 years. Mothers with 11 children received 5,000 roubles a year for the same period. Many women took up this offer, and in Moscow alone 2,730 families had more than eight children in 1936. The government also discouraged abortion, and in 1936 all abortions were banned except in cases were childbirth would endanger the life of the pregnant woman. Husbands who put pressure on their wives to have abortions, and doctors who performed illegal abortions, faced severe penalties.

Women were also expected to perform domestic duties such as cooking and cleaning. Indeed, during the 1930s, women spent five times longer on domestic labour than men. Inside the Communist Party, traditional gender roles were encouraged: men were expected to work, while women were expected to run a 'well ordered Communist home'. Communist women also took part in charitable work to improve the lives of their community. At Magnitogorsk, for example, the 'wife-activists movement' organised social events and the distribution of food to the needy. In theory, 'wife-activists' were expected to perform a mothering role to the entire community.

Family life

Stalin believed that the family was extremely important to society. Consequently, the Communists launched a propaganda campaign in the 1930s which **stigmatised** men who abandoned their wives and children.

Marriage was promoted during the 1930s. For example, wedding rings, which had been banned since 1928, were reintroduced in 1936. From 1936 onwards, marriage certificates were printed on high-quality paper to reflect the importance of marriage. Party members who married were given better accommodation and their own holiday homes, while members who had affairs were expelled from the party. Broadly speaking, these measures were successful. The 1937 census showed that 91% of men and 82% of women aged between 30 and 39 were married.

Sex outside marriage was discouraged. In 1934, the government launched an education campaign promoting sexual abstinence among young people. Police took action against young women who had an 'immoral' appearance, and collective farm chairmen performed medical virginity checks on young women. Incest, bigamy, adultery and male homosexuality were recriminalised.

The Soviet authorities made divorce less attractive, introducing new laws in 1936 which made the process more expensive. A first divorce would cost 50 roubles, the equivalent of one week's wages. A second divorce would cost 150 roubles. All subsequent divorces would cost 300 roubles. Finally, men who left their family were expected to contribute one-third of their earnings to support their children, or two-thirds of their earnings if they had three or more children.

Stalin's family policy aimed to make society more stable. Policy makers recognised that divorce and family break-up created economic and social problems. For example, single-parent families needed state aid which could otherwise be spent on industrial projects. Policy makers attempted to stabilise the family in order to maximise the amount of money available for industrialisation.

Education

Education stressed discipline, hard work and respect for authority in order to prepare young people for work in Russia's factories. To the same end, the curriculum was changed to emphasise traditional skills such as literacy and numeracy. The 1935 curriculum re-established a traditional syllabus for history. Students learnt about famous Russians, such as Ivan the Terrible, and the teaching emphasised Russian greatness. In this way, history teaching encouraged students to love their country and to respect figures of authority.

Outside school, young people learned the value of discipline through the Communist youth movement, the Komsomol. Its newspaper *Komsomolskaya Pravda* contained articles instructing children to show their parents respect and to work hard. Komsomol leaders praised Pavlik Morozov as the ideal child: hard-working, obedient and a committed Communist.

Conclusion

Stalin's social policy was designed to transform family life and education to serve the needs of a planned economy. The government therefore stressed stability, respect for authority, traditional skills such as literacy and numeracy and hard work, because these were the attributes which would help the economy to grow.

Glossary

'free love': the practice of having sexual relationships beyond, or independently of, marriage.
stigmatised: shamed or discredited.

Terror and propaganda in Stalin's Russia

Between 1935 and 1938, Stalin used the Communist secret police to persecute, arrest, torture, imprison or kill millions of Soviet citizens. This period, in which an estimated 3 million people died, is known as the Great Terror.

The origins of the Great Terror

Lenin's precedent

Terror had been part of the Communist system since 1917. Within a month of the revolution, Lenin had established the Cheka, an organisation dedicated to destroying the enemies of the Communist Party. During the Civil War it used surveillance, torture and murder to ensure the survival of the Communist government. In the early 1920s, the Communist secret police used its power to destroy the last remnants of opposition political parties. For example, in 1922 the government organised a public trial of the surviving leaders of the socialist parties which had opposed the Communists during the Civil War. In one sense, Stalin followed the pattern of terror set by Lenin, but with the new twist of using it to attack the Communist Party itself.

The leadership struggle

Stalin's motives for unleashing terror on the Communist Party go back to the leadership struggles of the 1920s, which had shown how easy it was to lose power. Trotsky, Zinoviev, Kamenev and Bukharin had all been leading figures in the party, but had all fallen from grace. Stalin worried that he might face the same fate. He used terror to consolidate his position and to ensure that his former rivals could no longer threaten him.

Economic solutions

Stalin also used terror for economic reasons. First, he imprisoned or executed economic managers and workers, blaming them for the failures of his Five-Year Plans. Second, he needed a bigger workforce to implement the Five-Year Plans, and the large prison population created by the Terror provided a cheap labour reserve. In this way, the Terror provided a scapegoat for the failings of his economic plans, and the slave labour necessary to ensure future targets were met.

The Congress of Victors, 1934

The 1934 Communist Party Congress was the first gathering of the party since Stalin's assumption of power. It was designed to celebrate the successes of Stalin's policies.

Nonetheless, Sergei Kirov, the moderate leader of the Leningrad party, gained a higher vote than Stalin in elections to the Central Committee, receiving 1,225 votes to Stalin's 927. Senior Communists privately invited Kirov to stand against Stalin for the party leadership. Kirov refused, and the true voting figures were covered up, but Stalin became extremely suspicious of the party members gathered at the Congress. He turned on the party, and within 3 years of the Congress over half of the delegates had been killed.

Stalin's paranoia

Stalin knew that he had used devious means to come to power. He also knew that some within the party knew of Lenin's *Testament* and its request that Stalin be sacked. He was aware that Trotsky had a more heroic record, that Bukharin was a better theorist, and that Zinoviev and Kamenev had been closer to Lenin. It has been argued that Stalin suffered from an **inferiority complex** and did not trust the people who knew or suspected the truth about how he had risen to power.

Genrikh Yagoda, a leading figure in Russia's secret police, sought to win favour with Stalin by pandering to his fears. Yagoda gave Stalin frequent reports of conspiracies against him within the Red Army, the Communist Party and the secret police. Stalin did not fully trust the Red Army, as it had been led by Trotsky until 1925, nor did he fully trust the party or the secret police, both of which had been established by Lenin. This paranoia is undoubtedly one explanation of the terror that Stalin launched in the mid-1930s.

Kirov's murder

The murder of Kirov in December 1934 at his party headquarters in Leningrad was the catalyst for the Great Terror. The murder was convenient for Stalin because it removed his most powerful rival and allowed him to claim that the Communist Party was under attack. Stalin imprisoned leading members of the Leningrad party and his old opponents Zinoviev and Kamenev, claiming that they had murdered Kirov on Trotsky's orders. By early 1935, again using Kirov's murder as the pretext, Stalin had extended the arrests throughout Russia.

The course of the Great Terror

Purges under Yagoda and the NKVD, 1934–36

The Great Terror started in Leningrad. Within months of Kirov's murder, between 30,000 and 40,000 people had been arrested. Stalin claimed they were part of a huge conspiracy organised by Trotsky, Zinoviev and Kamenev. He sent a letter to Communist Party secretaries throughout the country asking them to hunt down and arrest 'Trotskyites'. He called this letter 'Lessons of the events connected with the evil murder of Comrade Kirov'.

Stalin instructed Yagoda, now leader of the secret police, to prepare evidence against Zinoviev, Kamenev, Bukharin and their supporters for a forthcoming trial to link them with Kirov's murder.

In 1936, Yagoda organised the Trial of the Sixteen. The first of three Moscow **show trials**, it was designed to publicly humiliate Stalin's former rivals and to give Stalin the authority to execute his enemies. The Trial of the Sixteen featured 16 prominent party leaders, including Zinoviev and Kamenev. The defendants were accused of murdering Kirov, plotting to assassinate Stalin, sabotaging collectivisation and the First Five-Year Plan and plotting with Trotsky and foreign powers to overthrow the Communist government. Yagoda persuaded the Sixteen to confess by promising them that if they did, their lives would be spared. However, at the end of the trial they were condemned to death and shot.

Yezhovshchina, 1936–38

Stalin was dissatisfied with the progress of the Terror under Yagoda. He believed that the secret police were not arresting people fast enough and were slow in forcing prisoners to confess. For example, Yagoda had ordered the deaths of only 1,118 people in 1936. Moreover, Stalin knew that Yagoda had been a supporter of Bukharin in 1928 and so was extremely suspicious when Yagoda failed to put Bukharin on trial in 1936. Stalin sacked Yagoda and replaced him with Nikolai Yezhov.

Yezhov streamlined the Terror system. First, he replaced many of the old members of the secret police who had been recruited by Lenin and felt considerable loyalty to the Communist Party and the first generation of revolutionary leaders. Yezhov's new recruits did not have these loyalties and were therefore more willing to turn against members of the party. Additionally, the new members of the secret police were more willing to use torture. Yezhov introduced the 'conveyor belt' system of interrogation whereby suspects were subjected to sleep deprivation and torture round the clock until they confessed.

Stalin and Yezhov created a new system for managing the Terror, based on the Five-Year Plans. Stalin announced that the secret police were 'four years behind' in their mission to root out opposition. Targets for the number of arrests were set centrally and secret police action was then based on these targets. Notably, senior members of the secret police complained that the targets were too low, so they were increased. Yezhov's methods took over all aspects of life, and had such an impact that the Russian people gave his name to the Terror, calling it Yezhovshchina ('the Yezhov era').

Yezhov organised the second of the Moscow show trials, the Trial of the Seventeen (1937). This trial dealt with many of Trotsky's former allies. Once again, the defendants were charged with Kirov's murder, plotting to overthrow Stalin and the Communist government, economic sabotage, and collaborating with Trotsky. The evidence on which the trial was based was clearly fabricated. For example, one of the defendants confessed to murdering Kirov despite being in prison when it happened. The Trial of the Seventeen, like the Trial of the Sixteen, ended with guilty verdicts for all the defendants. They were either executed or sent to prison camps, where they died shortly after the trial.

Yezhov's final service to Stalin was the last Moscow show trial, the Trial of the Twenty-One (1938), featuring Bukharin and his supporter Rykov. The charges were very similar to those of the first two show trials, with the exception that Bukharin was also accused of attempting to assassinate Lenin. Bukharin broke with tradition by refusing to confess to all the crimes of which he was accused and by denying conspiracy against Lenin. The trial was also different in that Bukharin was not tortured. Instead, Stalin threatened to kill his wife and his newborn child. At the end of the trial Bukharin and his one-time supporters were sentenced to death.

Terror under Beria, 1938–53

Lavrenti Beria took over the secret police after Yezhov resigned in 1938. Following the Trial of the Twenty-One, the Great Terror subsided, but Beria continued to use terror as a weapon against Stalin's enemies. Beria's first big campaign was against Yezhov and his associates. A little over a year after the Trial of the Twenty-One, Yezhov himself was arrested by the secret police. Yezhov claimed that his only crime was killing too few Russians. In February 1940, he was executed along with 346 of his closest colleagues.

A year later, following the outbreak of war with Germany, Stalin turned his attention to the army and military intelligence. Stalin claimed that they were at fault for not anticipating the German invasion and for failing to defend Russia. The secret police were also used to deal with Soviet citizens that Stalin did not trust. Specifically, they targeted non-Russian ethnic groups that might welcome Germany's invasion because they wanted to be free of Russian rule. The secret police were given the job of transporting entire populations from the country's west, where the Germans were invading, to the east, where they posed no threat to Stalin. The treatment was brutal. For example, over 130,000 Kalmyks were forcibly deported to Siberia and by 1953, only 53,000 survived. Similarly, Beria ordered 460,000 Chechens to be deported in just 7 days. Harsh weather and Chechen resistance made this impossible, so the Chechen people who had not been deported were locked in large barns and burned alive.

Following the Second World War the secret police were ordered to deal with the 1.5 million Soviet citizens who had been captured by the Germans. These **prisoners of war** were treated as traitors and sent to gulags. Their labour also helped to rebuild Russia after the devastating war.

A second post-war campaign was the purge of the Jews. Stalin was suspicious of Russians who had contact with the outside world, fearing that they were spies. Indeed, he disliked any Russian who was loyal to anything other than the Soviet state. Stalin believed that the Jews were loyal to other Jews rather than to Russia. Consequently, between 1945 and 1951 Jews in important positions were removed. In 1945, 12% of high-level managers in the government and industry were Jewish, but by 1951 this had fallen to 4%. All the Jews working in sensitive areas such as diplomacy and the military were removed.

The Leningrad Affair was the last major purge under Stalin. Stalin believed that Communists in Leningrad acted with considerable independence. Indeed, the city had been a powerbase for Zinoviev and Kirov, two of his most important rivals. In 1949 Stalin ordered Beria to investigate the Communists in the city. This resulted in 1,000 party members being sacked, 200 of whom were arrested and charged with treason. The Leningrad Affair was extremely worrying for the Communist Party. The Great Terror of the 1930s had started in Leningrad and many were concerned that the Leningrad Affair would lead to another wave of terror.

The so-called Doctors' Plot was the final wave of terror unleashed by Stalin. In 1952 his doctor, Professor Vladimir Vinogradov, recommended that Stalin reduce his workload because of his ill-health and old age. In response Stalin accused him and 30 senior doctors of plotting to assassinate leading Communists. Fortunately, Stalin died prior to their execution, so they all survived. Beria was arrested 4 months after Stalin's death and was executed for treason at the end of 1953.

The consequences of the Great Terror

Political consequences

The Great Terror had a dramatic effect on the Communist Party. Between 1934 and 1938, 330,000 party members were convicted of being enemies of the people. Many of those executed were the first generation of revolutionaries who had participated in the revolution and the Civil War. By destroying these people Stalin removed everyone who knew anything about his rise to power. The show trials were particularly important because they finally eliminated his rivals: Zinoviev, Kamenev, Bukharin and many others who had been close to Lenin and who therefore had authority that was independent of Stalin. The fact that they were convicted of treason allowed Stalin to claim that he was the only Communist leader who could be trusted.

Stalin also used terror against the Red Army, which he did not trust because the majority of its senior officers had been appointed by Trotsky. Stalin's purge of the army started with the secret trial of Marshal Mikhail Tukhachevsky in June 1937. Confessions were obtained by torture, and in the following 18 months 34,000 soldiers were purged from the army. This purge, like the purge of the party, was part of Stalin's continuing attempt to consolidate his position.

At a local level the Terror swept away managers and politicians and replaced them with new leaders who were more loyal to Stalin. Stakhanovites were highly active during the purges, many holding meetings in which they criticised their managers, and some organising local show trials to humiliate factory bosses. The senior ranks of Soviet industry became the scapegoats for economic problems and were sacked for being 'wreckers' or handed over to the secret police.

Social consequences

After the first show trial the secret police claimed that as many as a quarter of a million Russians were involved in the anti-Communist conspiracy. Many ordinary people collaborated with the secret police in rooting out spies and enemies of the government. Some tried to avoid being sent to prison by denouncing their friends and neighbours and thereby proving their loyalty to the party. In 1937, 353,074 Russians were executed and 429,311 were sent to prison camps. It is estimated that 10% of the country's men were either executed or sent to gulags during the Great Terror.

Significantly, the Terror affected some groups more than others. For example, 95% of the victims of the Terror were men, while just 5% were women. It affected the urban and educated population much more than manual workers or peasants. Those most at risk were between the ages of 30 and 45, in managerial or professional positions. At the height of the Terror in 1937, many of the apartment blocks in central Moscow which housed senior Communist officials were deserted. The Great Terror also discriminated on the basis of nationality: the secret police had specific targets for the numbers of Poles, Romanians and Latvians to be persecuted.

Economic consequences

The Terror had a devastating effect on the Russian economy. Purges within Gosplan eliminated many of Russia's most experienced economic planners. Similarly, purges of local factory managers swept away many experienced and competent people. The Terror thus made effective economic management very difficult. The effects of the Terror on Gosplan meant that the Third Five-Year Plan was never published and managers were forced to work with drafts. The chaos that the Terror caused in the economy is clear from the results of the Third Five-Year Plan. The Donbas coalmines, for example, accounted for over three-quarters of Russia's coal production. Between the summer of 1936 and the autumn of 1938, more than a quarter of the managers in the mines were purged. As a result, the rate of coal production, which had doubled between 1928 and 1932 and again between 1932 and 1936, barely grew from the beginning of the Great Terror to 1940.

History, propaganda and art

Terror was not the only means of social control in Stalin's Russia. The leader also used propaganda, art and specially rewritten histories to ensure the loyalty of his people.

Socialist Realism

Stalin's advisors on art argued that Soviet art should adopt a style that they called Socialist Realism. This term emerged in 1932 at the first All-Union Congress of Soviet Writers. Various definitions of Socialist Realism were put forward. For example, Ivan

Kulik defined it as art that provided 'a true reflection of reality' and helped 'the building of socialism'. Others argued that Socialist Realism was art that was full of *partynost* (the spirit of the party), *narodnost* (the spirit of the nation) and *ideynost* (new Communist thinking).

In practice, Socialist Realist art focused on Communist government policy, and so pictures and sculptures were made depicting collectivisation and the Five-Year Plans. Additionally, Socialist Realist art was realistic in the sense that it aimed to look like a photograph.

Paintings

Generally speaking, Socialist Realist paintings had three themes. First, pictures portrayed Communist leaders. For example, there were many portraits of Stalin. Significantly, many of these, such as *Leader, Teacher, Friend* by G. Shegal and *Stalin's Speech at the Sixteenth Congress of the Communist Party* by A. M. Gerasimov, included Stalin in the foreground and Lenin in the background. This implied that Stalin was carrying on Lenin's work. Second, pictures portrayed happy villagers on collective farms. The paintings *To Mother for the Next Feed* by T. G. Gaponenko, showing peasants enjoying a bountiful meal, and *Voting to Expel the Kulak from the Collective Farm* by S. Adlivankin are two good examples of this. Third, paintings focused on the heroism of workers during the Five-Year Plans. A. V. Lobanov's *Training Cadres for Magnitostroi*, for example, shows a red specialist instructing a group of workers on the construction of a factory. Similarly, *Gold Mining* by N. F. Denisovsky shows hard-working members of the proletariat digging for gold in a quarry. These paintings were designed to inspire workers and peasants and to dignify the work they did.

Architecture

Socialist Realist architecture, like the paintings, was designed to be inspirational. For example, the Moscow metro stations, completed as part of the Five-Year Plans, were designed to look like palaces. Plans for the *Palace of Soviets*, which was never completed, included the highest tower in the world, topped with a 50-foot statue of Lenin. Between 1947 and 1953 Soviet builders completed seven elaborate skyscrapers in Moscow, which became known as Stalin's *Seven Sisters*. The architecture was designed to be **palatial** and impressive. It emphasised the grand scale of Stalin's vision.

Literature

Novels written during the 1930s were modelled on Fyodor Gladkov's *Cement*, written in 1924. *Cement* tells the story of a group of soldiers who leave the Red Army and build a cement works. Valentin Kataev's *Forward, Oh Time* (1934) tells a similar story about the construction of a steel works. These novels emphasised the heroic nature of Stalin's economic plans and were designed to inspire workers and peasants to follow him.

Propaganda

Many propaganda posters were produced during the 1930s. One important theme in Soviet propaganda was to reinforce Stalin's legitimacy as leader of the USSR. For example, the poster *Raise the Banner of Marx, Engels, Lenin and Stalin!* (1937) showed Stalin as the latest leader of a Communist tradition stretching all the way back to Karl Marx. Similarly, the poster *Under the Banner of Lenin for Social Construction* (1940) showed Stalin and Lenin together behind the construction projects of the Third Five-Year Plan. Propaganda posters also emphasised Stalin's industrial and agricultural policies. For example, *They are Talking About Us in Pravda* shows a group of peasants sitting with a Communist worker, surrounded by modern technology such as tractors and motorbikes. Finally, Soviet propaganda portrayed Stalin as 'the people's friend'. For example, *Thanks to Dear Stalin for a Happy, Joyful Childhood* (1937) shows Stalin embracing a child.

History

Soviet historians were given the job of rewriting Russian history in order to show that Stalin deserved to be the country's leader. For example, *The Short Course of the History of the All-Union Communist Party* (1938), which set out a history of the revolution and the Civil War, stressed Stalin's importance during every crucial period of the history of the Communist Party. Similarly, *The Short Biography of Stalin* (1938) only mentioned Trotsky, Zinoviev, Kamenev and Bukharin when discussing their treason. Both of these books, along with much Soviet art, put forward the 'Myth of the Two Leaders' which emphasised that Stalin had been Lenin's right-hand man and presented him as 'the Lenin of today'.

The cult of personality

During the 1930s, a 'cult of Stalin' emerged. Soviet propaganda attributed all the successes of the Communist government to Stalin. The newspaper *Pravda* praised Stalin's wisdom on a daily basis and party theorists began to write of a new ideology: Marxism-Leninism-Stalinism. Stalin's birthday was turned into a national celebration, involving marching troops and parades of children and workers. The cult emphasised that Stalin was not responsible for the problems of day-to-day life.

Conclusion

Stalin's regime has often been described as **totalitarian** because it attempted to exercise total control over its citizens. The Great Terror was one way in which Stalin attempted to control the people. Nonetheless, propaganda and art also played a significant role in inspiring people to support the regime.

Glossary

inferiority complex: a persistent feeling of inadequacy.

palatial: like a palace.

prisoners of war: soldiers captured by an opposing army in a time of war.

show trial: an event in which people are publicly shamed for criminal acts. The purpose of the trial is to make an example of the accused rather than to establish their guilt.

totalitarian: a form of government in which all aspects of life are brought under the control of the government, and in which citizens are expected to be enthusiastic supporters of the regime.

World war and Cold War: Stalin's Russia, 1945–51

Foreign policy, 1939–41

During the 1920s and 1930s, Russia had adopted a policy of **isolationism.** As the only Communist country in the world, it was unwilling to form alliances with capitalist nations. By 1936, however, **Hitler**'s military build-up in Germany left many countries anticipating a war. Stalin and other members of the Communist government believed that Hitler planned to attack the Soviet Union, as the Nazi leader's book *Mein Kampf* (1925) had criticised communism and explicitly stated that Germany needed to gain land from Russia in the east.

In 1939, Stalin signed a **pact** with Germany. The Nazi–Soviet pact committed Russia and Germany to work together and seek peace rather than resort to war to settle disagreements. The pact also contained a clause which was not made public at the time. Essentially, this secret clause gave Germany control of western Poland and Czechoslovakia, while Russia was free to pursue its own policies in Latvia, Lithuania and Estonia. A week after the pact was signed, Hitler invaded Poland and, by June 1940, Stalin had overthrown the governments of Latvia, Lithuania and Estonia.

Stalin assumed that war with Germany was inevitable and that Hitler would break the terms of the pact sooner or later. Stalin's reason for signing the pact was partly that it allowed him to retake territory that had once belonged to the Russian empire under the tsar, but also it helped his plan to put off war with Germany for as long as possible. In 1939, Russia was in no position to fight successfully against the Nazi war machine. The Great Terror had left Russia in economic turmoil, so Stalin wanted to buy time to prepare the country for war.

The Second World War

German invasion

In June 1941, Hitler launched Operation Barbarossa (Red Beard), an all-out attack on Russia focusing on Moscow and Leningrad. In September 1941, German forces reached the outskirts of Moscow. The attempt to take the city by force failed, leading the German army to **besiege** the city. In 1942, rather than concentrate on Moscow, Hitler sent new forces to capture the city of Stalingrad as part of Operation Blue, aimed at capturing Russia's oilfields. Once again, German forces tried to conquer the city but failed, instead keeping Stalingrad under siege.

The Soviet counter-attack

The Soviet counter-offensive, Operation Uranus, was launched in September 1942. By February 1943, German forces in Stalingrad had been surrounded and were forced to surrender. By December 1943 two-thirds of the territory captured by the Germans in their early offensives had been recaptured by Soviet forces. In early 1944, Stalin claimed 'ten great victories' which included recapturing Belarus, Latvia and Estonia. By January 1945 the Red Army was on German soil, and by April it had reached the outskirts of Germany's capital, Berlin. In May 1945, Germany surrendered to the **Allies**.

Reasons for Russia's victory

Russia's defeat of Germany was due to its economic strength, the dedication and heroism of its armed forces and civilian population, tactical decisions on the home front taken by Stalin, and the support of the Allies.

Economic strength

Gosplan, the organisation responsible for the Five Year Plans, was ideally suited to running a war economy. Russia's rearmament had started in 1936 during the Second Five-Year Plan, and had continued throughout the Third Five-Year Plan. During the war, Gosplan organised the relocation of industry from western parts of the country to the east, thus ensuring that it did not fall into Nazi hands. This was a highly complex task, but nevertheless 1,523 factories were taken apart and reassembled far to the east by November 1941. Gosplan was very successful in transforming the economy to meet the needs of war. By 1942, 50% of national income was being spent on the war, a much higher figure than that of Britain, Germany or the USA. Gosplan's efforts ensured that armaments production almost doubled between 1941 and 1944. This was a remarkable achievement, as throughout this period much of Russia's territory was in the hands of the Germans.

The role of the people

The Soviet people showed extraordinary dedication to supporting the war effort. Workers and peasants worked a 7-day week for the entire duration of the war. Factory shifts lasted between 10 and 12 hours, and workers were additionally expected to work a night shift on farms during the harvest season. Worker discipline was very strict: workers who arrived 20 minutes late could be handed over to military tribunals and tried.

Women bore the brunt of production during the war. In some regions, they made up as much as 75% of the workforce. On farms, the shortage of machinery meant that women were often required to perform tasks that should have been performed by machines or animals. In many areas, for example, women were yoked to ploughs in the absence of tractors or horses. In addition to working in factories or on farms, women were still expected to care for their families.

Young people were also required to contribute to the war effort. Those aged 14–17 were drafted into 'labour reserve schools' in which they were taught industrial skills necessary for war production.

The efforts of the civilian population were essential to the country's victory because they kept vital war industries going, ensuring that the armed forces had the supplies they needed to win the war.

Stalin's domestic policy

Stalin's pragmatic decisions on the **home front** were also essential for the USSR's victory. First, aware that socialism had not improved conditions for the majority of people and that many associated socialism with terror, he appealed to the Russian people's sense of nationalism rather than to the virtues of socialism. The war was referred to as 'the Great Patriotic War' and soldiers were encouraged to call the German enemy by nationalist and racist nicknames such as 'Hans', 'Fritz' and 'Kraut'. Alongside this revival of nationalism Stalin rehabilitated the role of the church in national life. The Russian Orthodox Church had traditionally played a major part in Russian identity, but the Communists had persecuted it. When war came, however, Stalin became more tolerant and granted Metropolitan Sergei (the church's most senior figure) an official residence in Moscow as well as promising greater freedom for church publications after the war. In return Metropolitan Sergei urged Christians to back Stalin, describing him as 'God's chosen leader'. The restoration of the church was very helpful for many of the troops too: as one solider noted, a few of Jesus' words were more comforting in the face of death than the complete works of Marx, Lenin and Stalin put together.

The support of the Allies

Russia's allies helped the country to emerge victorious by preventing Germany from concentrating all its military resources on the eastern front. Germany had to split its forces, with some fighting the Allies in the west and some fighting Russia in the east. After **D-Day** in 1944 there were actually three fronts in the war: the Western Allies were fighting Germany across France in the west, another campaign raged in Italy, and the Russians were fighting the Nazis in the east.

The Allies were also able to provide aid to Russia through the Lend-Lease programme. Initially set up by the Americans to help the UK, this scheme was extended to the Russians once they entered the war in 1941. In overall terms Gosplan estimated that 4% of the goods used in the war came from the Lend-Lease scheme. In terms of military equipment this included 12% of the aeroplanes, 10% of the tanks and 2% of the artillery used in the war. The aid was more significant in terms of food and transport, two areas in which the Soviet economy was weak. American food provided approximately 17% of the calories consumed by Soviet soldiers each day. Equally, two-thirds of the jeeps used by the Russians came from the USA. Thus while Lend-Lease supplied only a limited amount of the total goods used in the war, it did help strategically, making up for the areas in which the Russian economy was weak. In this sense it was significant for the Russian victory.

The cost of the war

The war took a tremendous toll on the Soviet economy and people. It has been estimated that the war effort effectively wiped out the economic advances made during the first three Five-Year Plans. By 1942 the Germans had control of one-third of Russian agriculture and industry. Additionally, approximately 12 million men who would otherwise have worked in Russian farms and factories were drafted into the armed forces. For both of these reasons there was a dramatic downturn in production. Soviet citizens were sustained on the barest of rations, as 90% of farm produce was taken by the government and diverted to the war effort. Russians who lived through the sieges of Moscow, Leningrad and Stalingrad had to live on whatever they could find. The citizens of Leningrad lived on 'blockade bread', made largely of sawdust; they also ate birds, rats and pets, and in some cases resorted to cannibalism.

The Russians and the Germans both adopted a scorched earth policy: while the Germans were advancing, the Russians were required to destroy any equipment or supplies that might fall into German hands, and when the Germans were retreating they destroyed anything left behind that might aid the Russians. Consequently 25% of Russia's pre-war industrial equipment and 32,000 factories were destroyed. In agriculture, 70,000 villages were destroyed, while in terms of transportation, 65,000 km of railway track were destroyed. Thus Russia's victory was achieved at great cost to her people, her industry and her farmland.

Russia's emergence as a superpower

Following the Second World War, Russia emerged as a superpower. This status was based on the country's economic might, its influence in Europe and its possession of the atomic bomb.

Russia's economy was shattered by the Second World War. Nonetheless, the Fourth Five-Year Plan, launched in 1946, made it the fastest-growing in the world. Stalin used the economic growth to increase military spending. In 1945 alone, Gosplan allocated 7.4 billion roubles to defence spending, compared with 5.7 million in 1940. Heavy industry recovered quickly, and by 1952 total industrial output was twice that of 1940. By the end of the Fourth Plan in 1950, steel production was 49% above the 1940 figure and coal production was 57% higher. As ever, consumer goods were not a priority and living standards remained at the 1930 level. This, however, had little bearing on the country's superpower status, as the continuing emphasis on heavy industry ensured that the economy was well placed to fight another war.

Russia's control of Eastern Europe following the war also put it in a position of much greater influence. Allied leaders had agreed that Russia should have a **sphere of influence** in the east. In practice this meant that it used the Red Army to established Communist governments in newly liberated countries such as Czechoslovakia, Hungary and Poland. The governments were modelled on the Soviet government — they were dominated by the Communist Party and a powerful secret police force. Russia organised trade relations in Eastern Europe through an organisation called Comecon (the Council for Mutual Economic Assistance), established in 1949, which ensured Russia was the prime beneficiary of the trade deals.

Russia was also recognised as a superpower because of its nuclear capacity. The USA had developed a nuclear bomb towards the end of the Second World War and had demonstrated its effectiveness by bombing Hiroshima and Nagasaki. Stalin recognised the significance of the new weapon and tasked a team of scientists with producing a Russian nuclear bomb. East Germany and Czechoslovakia, both of which were part of the Soviet sphere of influence, had large deposits of radioactive uranium, which was essential for building the first generation of nuclear bombs. By 1949 the Russian team, lead by Igor Kurchatov, had produced their own bomb, which was nicknamed Joe-1 by the Americans, a reference to Stalin's first name, Joseph. By 1953 the Russians had also developed 'Layer Cake', a hydrogen bomb, which was an even more destructive type of nuclear weapon.

Russia's economic strength, influence in Eastern Europe and possession of the nuclear bomb were all crucial ingredients in the country's emergence as a superpower following the Second World War. By Stalin's death in 1953 it was clear that the USA and Russia had eclipsed the empires that had dominated the world prior to the war. The post-war world would be dominated by the two new superpowers.

Glossary

Allies: an alliance of the UK, France, the USA and Russia during the Second World War.

besiege: to surround a city with military forces with the aim of forcing it to surrender by starving its citizens into submission.

D-Day: 6 June 1944, the day on which Allied forces began the invasion of France in the Second World War.

Hitler: the leader of Nazi Germany from 1933 to 1945.

home front: the activities of civilians during a war.

isolationism: a policy of remaining isolated from the affairs of other countries.

pact: an agreement.

sphere of influence: a geographical area over which one nation exercises political and economic influence.

Questions
&
Answers

This section contains five specimen exam questions. Two specimen answers are given for each question: an A-grade and a C-grade response. At the end of each answer are detailed examiner comments, preceded by the icon ℮, explaining how and why marks have been awarded.

When exam papers are marked, all answers are given a level of response and then a precise numerical mark. Answers are awarded one of five levels:
- **level 1**: 1–6 marks
- **level 2**: 7–12 marks
- **level 3**: 13–18 marks
- **level 4**: 19–24 marks
- **level 5**: 25–30 marks

Question 1

Why did Stalin emerge as leader of Russia in 1928–29?

■ ■ ■

A-grade answer

There were many reasons why Stalin became leader of Soviet Russia in 1928. The most important reason was the institutions that gave him power. However, ideological debates about the economy, the impact of Lenin on Soviet political life, and shifting alliances also played a part.

One reason why Stalin emerged as leader was the political institutions that he headed. His roles within the party gave him the power to appoint, promote and sack party members. For example, as General Secretary, a role he was given in 1922, he had the power of patronage and could appoint people to prestigious jobs. He was also able to select who attended Party Congresses. Since Party Congresses were used to select the Central Committee, Stalin had a powerful influence over the leadership of the party. Through the Lenin Enrolment he recruited members of the Communist Party, and as head of the Workers' and Peasants' Inspectorate he had the power to sack party members. In contrast, Stalin's opponents had little institutional power. Zinoviev and Kamenev had only local leadership roles and Trotsky was leader of the Red Army but still inferior to the leaders of the Communist Party. In this way, Stalin had power over the lower and upper ranks of the party and used this to gain support in the leadership struggle.

Another reason why Stalin emerged as leader was the ideological debates about economic policy. Originally, Stalin had been committed to continuing the NEP. This gained him popularity within the party, as the NEP solved the problems created by War Communism and also helped Russia's industry to prosper. In contrast, Trotsky supported rapid industrialisation. He wanted the government to control the economy and to use all the wealth generated to develop industry as quickly as possible. To this end he said that agriculture should be collectivised. This was unpopular with the peasants, as they wanted to have control of their own farms. Consequently, Trotsky and the Left Opposition were unpopular in the party. In 1928 Stalin switched his allegiance to support collectivisation. This gained him a lot of support within the party because by this time the NEP was seen to be failing. The ideological debates were important to Stalin's rise to power because he was able to use them to gain popularity within the party.

A third factor that explains Stalin's rise to power was Lenin's impact on Soviet politics. Lenin had created a highly centralised government and had banned all other political parties. He had also banned members of the party from opposing the party leadership through the 1921 ban on factions. Stalin was able to use this system to remove his rivals from power by accusing them of factionalism. Additionally, Stalin was able to

use Lenin's writings to gain power. Lenin's writings were often vague and seemed to contradict themselves. Stalin was able to claim that his ideology was the same as Lenin's. Stalin was able to use Lenin's politics and ideology to gain power because Lenin had left behind a political system and political ideas that Stalin was able to exploit.

Finally, Stalin cleverly used alliances to gain power. For example, between 1923 and 1925 he was a member of the Triumvirate. He used this alliance with Zinoviev and Kamenev to defeat Trotsky in important party debates. He also told Trotsky the wrong date for Lenin's funeral, allowing the Triumvirate to claim that Trotsky was absent because he did not respect Lenin. These methods were successful, and in 1925 Trotsky's economic policies were rejected by the Party Congress. Stalin then switched alliances, collaborating with Bukharin to defeat Zinoviev and Kamenev. Stalin ensured that the 1927 Party Congress was filled with his supporters, while Bukharin gave excellent speeches explaining why Zinoviev and Kamenev's policies were wrong. For this reason, Zinoviev and Kamenev were expelled from the party. Finally, Stalin turned on Bukharin. He rejected the NEP and used his support in the party to enforce collectivisation in Russia. In 1929 Bukharin was expelled from the Politburo. Stalin used alliances to achieve power because they allowed him to pick off his opponents in turn rather than dealing with all of them at once.

In conclusion, Stalin became leader of Soviet Russia through a combination of institutional, ideological, historical and tactical factors. However, the most important factor was institutional. Stalin's roles within the party gave him great influence and allowed him to capitalise on the ideological debates and the structure of the party that Lenin had left behind.

> This essay offers an analytical response which focuses well on the question. It discusses a series of issues that are central to Stalin's emergence as leader. It supports these with accurate detail and links them clearly to the question. In the conclusion, it states which factor was the most important. It reaches Level 5 because of the sustained nature of the analysis.

Level 5: 28/30

C-grade answer

Stalin's character was unremarkable. He was outshone by Trotsky's oratory, Bukharin's intellect, and the status of Zinoviev and Kamenev as Lenin's closest friends. Nonetheless, Trotsky's and Bukharin's brilliance alienated many within the party, whereas Stalin's 'greyness' became his greatest strength.

Stalin's background was better suited to understanding the hopes and fears of the Russian Communists. Stalin, like many in the Communist Party, was brought up in a poor family. He had little knowledge of the Western world or of other languages and cultures. He was not an intellectual. Because of this, members of the Communist Party were able to identify with him. Stalin also appeared unthreatening, particularly compared to Trotsky. Trotsky was clearly ambitious, a military leader, a gifted orator, and looked like a potential dictator. Stalin, on the other hand, was just an administrator. As General Secretary, he appeared to threaten no one. In spite of this, Stalin was willing to do anything to take power, sacrificing old friendships with Zinoviev, Kamenev and then Bukharin in order to gain the advantage. One of Stalin's great gifts was his ability to hide his ambition and appear to be a 'grey blur'.

Stalin's opponents were much weaker. After the Civil War, Trotsky found it difficult to win support within the Communist Party. Bukharin's youthfulness led many within the Central Committee to feel he was too immature to take power.

Stalin was much stronger than his opponents and that is why he won.

e This answer lists Stalin's strengths in one paragraph and his opponents' weaknesses in another. It is detailed but the focus on the question is largely implicit and there is no real analysis or explanation. It also lacks balance and therefore does not reach the top of Level 3.

Level 3: 18/30

Question 2

How successful were Stalin's economic policies, 1929–41?

■ ■ ■

A-grade answer

Stalin's economic policies were partially successful. He succeeded in increasing the production of raw materials for heavy industry, and in boosting labour productivity. However, his plans to transform agriculture and rearm in preparation for war were much less successful.

In terms of agriculture, Stalin's economic policies were far from successful. Stalin aimed to collectivise the country's farms and produce enough grain to feed his workers and fund industrialisation. Stalin did not succeed in collectivising all farms. Indeed, following Stalin's 'Dizzy with Success' article in 1930, the number of collective farms decreased. In March 1930, 50% of farms were collectivised, but by August 1930, only 25% remained collectivised. Similarly, Stalin failed to increase grain production. Ten million peasants were exiled between 1929 and 1931, and this drop in the workforce led to a fall in agricultural production. By 1932, agricultural production was so low that there was a famine in the countryside and a severe lack of food in the cities. Clearly, Stalin's agricultural policies cannot be viewed as a success.

All three Five-Year Plans focused on heavy industry, and Stalin was successful in his aim of increasing the production of steel, coal and iron. During the First Five-Year Plan, oil production increased from 11.7 million tonnes in 1929 to 21.4 million tonnes in 1932. Similarly, coal production increased from 35.4 million tonnes to 64.3 million tonnes in this period. The Second Five-Year Plan built on these successes, trebling the production of steel. Although the production of crude oil and steel stagnated under the Third Five-Year Plan, production of coal increased from 128 million tonnes in 1937 to 166 million tonnes in 1940. However, these figures disguised the low quality of many of the raw materials produced. Additionally, they hid the fact that many managers exaggerated how much they had produced in order to avoid being sent to gulags. In this way, Stalin successfully increased the production of raw materials, but was less successful in meeting his targets and producing materials that could be used for manufacturing.

The Second Five-Year Plan also aimed to increase labour productivity. Alexei Stakhanov successfully mined 227 tonnes of coal in a single shift and was rewarded with luxuries such as a new flat, a telephone and cinema tickets. His example inspired other workers, who were similarly rewarded for exceeding targets. Female agricultural worker Maria Demchenko followed Stakhanov's example, bringing in four times the average harvest of sugar beet. In this way, the Stakhanovite movement was successful in increasing labour productivity within Russia and contributed to the increased production of raw materials.

In terms of rearmament and preparation for war, there was mixed success. The Plans were successful in devoting economic resources to rearmament. Under the Second Five-Year Plan, defence spending rose from 4% of government expenditure in 1933 to 17% in 1937. In the period of the Third Five-Year Plan, military spending doubled. By 1940, a third of all investment went to the armed forces. In addition, increases in the production of heavy industry were important as iron, steel, coal and oil were vital for weapons manufacture. However, Stalin's purges removed many experienced managers from overseeing the rearmament process, while the low quality of many of the raw materials made them unusable for the production of weapons. Consequently, Russia remained far from prepared for the onset of war.

In conclusion, Stalin's economic policies were partly successful. Heavy industry grew massively, aided by an increase in labour productivity during the Second Five-Year Plan. On the other hand, Stalin failed to transform agriculture and boost grain production. Similarly, although production of raw materials rose, the low quality of these raw materials prevented them from being useful for rearmament and hindered Stalin's aim of preparing for war.

🖉 Throughout this essay, the focus is on the extent to which Stalin's economic policy was successful. This is addressed in terms of a series of themes. In this sense, it offers an analytical answer which directly addresses the question. The essay contains a great deal of factual material which helps to establish the extent to which Stalin's policies can be considered a success. The essay is consistently logical and reaches a coherent judgement that is supported by the preceding argument.

Level 5: 27/30

C-grade answer

The Russian economy in 1929 was in a mess. From 1914 to 1921 the country was involved in war almost all of the time. The First World War and then the Civil War wrecked the economy. Before this, Russia's economy was never very good compared to the western world. The NEP brought about growth between 1921 and 1926, but in 1927 there were new problems, which led Stalin to adopt new radical policies such as collectivisation and the Five-Year Plans.

Agricultural policy was not very successful. The NEP had let agriculture run in a capitalist way, with small farms making money through growing crops and selling them for a profit. But the Communists were against capitalism, so when the NEP started failing with the grain procurement crisis the Communists decided the time had come to liquidate the kulaks. The kulaks were rich peasants who the government said were capitalists forcing the price of grain up through the kulak grain strike. To deal with this the Communists sent troops into the countryside and captured or killed the rich peasants. In total 10 million peasants were sent to labour camps for being kulaks. The 'Liquidation of the Kulaks' was the end of the NEP and the end of capitalism in the countryside.

question

Collectivisation was the new policy that replaced the NEP. It meant that small farms joined together into big farms which were state-owned. The Communists hoped that collectivisation would boost production by 50%, but this did not happen. A famine broke out, and between 1932 and 1934 10 million people starved to death. The famine was known as the Great Famine. In the cities too there was not much food and Stalin had to introduce rationing.

The First-Five-Year Plan was very successful. For example, iron production increased from 3.3 million tonnes in 1928 to 6.2 million tonnes in 1932. Steel production also increased by almost 2 million tonnes during the plan. The production of coal and oil almost doubled during the plan. What is more, there was an increase in urbanisation as peasants left the villages to work in the new factories. This is what the Communists wanted, because they thought they were the party of the working class.

Overall, Stalin's economic policy was very successful because it liquidated the kulaks, increased production and raised productivity through the Stakhanovite movement.

📝 This essay contains a great deal of relevant detail and therefore gets a high mark within Level 3. Nonetheless, it is poorly focused on the question. The introduction gives the background rather than answering the question, and the second paragraph addresses why Stalin's policies were introduced rather than how successful they were. Finally, the paragraph on industrial policy and the conclusion are very one-sided, as they focus on the successes and ignore the failings of Stalin's policies.

Level 3: 17/30

Question 3

How accurate is it to describe Soviet social policy in the 1930s as a 'Great Retreat'?

■ ■ ■

A-grade answer

During the 1930s, Stalin introduced policies affecting women, the family and education. Trotsky thought that these policies were more traditional than those promoted by the Communists in the 1920s, and therefore he labelled Stalin's social policy the 'Great Retreat'. In terms of policy towards the family and education, Trotsky's description was entirely correct. However, in terms of policy towards women, the description is too simplistic.

In many ways, Stalin's social policy did signal a 'Great Retreat' for women. Under Lenin, women had enjoyed state-provided childcare, the right to abortion on demand, and the right to divorce their husbands. Under Stalin, however, many women were forced to adopt the more traditional roles of housewives and mothers. For example, Communist Party guidelines stated that women were expected to run a 'well ordered Communist home', and during the 1930s, women spent five times longer on household duties, such as cooking and cleaning, than men. In addition, the Communist Party introduced rewards for women with large families. Women who had seven children received 2,000 roubles a year for 5 years, while mothers with 11 children received 5,000 roubles a year for the same period. In 1936, the government also criminalised abortion in all cases except those where the mother's life was in danger.

In spite of these measures, there was one respect in which Stalin's policy towards women could be viewed as progressive: he encouraged many women to join the workforce. For example, between 1928 and 1940, 10 million women joined the industrial workforce. Similarly, by 1945, 80% of collective farm workers were women, as were two of the country's most well-known agricultural Stakhanovites — Pasha Angelina and Maria Demchenko. Furthermore, the Communist government increased the number of places for women in higher and technical education, from 20% in 1929 to 40% in 1940.

Stalin thus rejected many of the progressive measures introduced during the 1920s and re-emphasised traditional roles for women. However, at the same time, he encouraged women into paid employment. It is therefore only partially accurate to describe his policy towards women as a 'Great Retreat'.

Stalin's policy towards the family was more clearly a 'Great Retreat'. Stalin believed that marriage stabilised society and he used a number of measures to encourage people to marry and stay married. In 1936, he reintroduced wedding rings and allowed marriage certificates to be printed on high-quality paper. At the same time, he introduced high fees for divorce. For example, a first divorce would cost 50 roubles, a second divorce 150 roubles, and all subsequent divorces 300 roubles. Further to

this, party members who were married were rewarded with better accommodation and holiday homes. In addition, Stalin discouraged sex outside marriage. Party members who had affairs were expelled from the party, while the chairmen of collective farms were encouraged to perform medical virginity checks on young women. Incest, bigamy, adultery and male homosexuality were recriminalised. Stalin's policy towards the family thus rejected the 'free love' attitude of the 1920s and in this respect deserves to be called a 'Great Retreat'.

In terms of education, Stalin also focused on traditional values. He believed that students should be disciplined, hard-working and respectful. To this end, he used the *Komsomol*, the Communist youth movement, to instruct children to respect their parents and teachers and to be loyal to Communist ideals. Within schools, traditional skills such as literacy and numeracy were stressed. In addition, students devoted time to learning about famous Russians such as Ivan the Terrible. In many ways this contradicted policy introduced in the 1920s. During this period, students had studied a more revolutionary curriculum and had been encouraged to see themselves as the equal of their parents and teachers. For this reason, Stalin's education policy can indeed be viewed as a 'Great Retreat'.

Overall, the majority of Stalin's social policies can be described as a 'Great Retreat'. He rejected much of the sexual and educational equality promoted by the Communists in the 1920s. Instead, he created policies designed to emphasise traditional roles and relationships, stressing that women should be good housewives and mothers, that marriage was essential for a stable society, and that students should respect their elders. In one respect only did Stalin's policy suggest progression — he encouraged women to take employment in industry or agriculture. However, this is perhaps less evidence of a progressive viewpoint, and more evidence that Stalin was not prepared to let his social policy jeopardise the achievement of his economic goals.

🖉 This essay answers the question in a logical and analytical manner. It analyses in the sense that it breaks social policy down into three categories: women, family and education. It is logical because it deals with them in turn, and develops a complete argument out of the different aspects of social policy. At every turn, the essay establishes criteria against which it judges the accuracy of the claim that Stalin's social policy was a 'Great Retreat'.

Level 5: 30/30

C-grade answer

In the 1930s, Stalin introduced many policies that affected women, families and education. It is largely correct to describe Stalin's social policy as a 'Great Retreat'.

In much of his policy towards women Stalin did emphasise traditional values, and in this respect it is accurate to say that his policy was a 'Great Retreat'. For example, he gave women rewards for having lots of children. He also told them to ensure that they kept their homes clean and their families well fed. Additionally, he tried to make women become involved in charity work. On the other hand, Stalin did encourage women to join the workforce, and many of them did. Some worked in factories and some in agriculture. In this way, Stalin's policy towards women was a 'Great Retreat' to an extent, as it encouraged women to have traditional roles but also gave them opportunities to get jobs.

In his policy towards families, Stalin also emphasised traditional values. For example, he encouraged people to get married by offering them incentives. In addition, he made it expensive to get divorced. He also encouraged people not to have sex outside marriage. He punished people who had affairs, suggested that young people avoid having sex altogether and made it illegal to be homosexual. Stalin's policy towards families was definitely a 'Great Retreat', as it reversed many of the changes the Communists had brought about in the 1920s.

In terms of education, Stalin's policy can also be called a 'Great Retreat'. He told students to be respectful, and also checked that they could read well and were good at maths. In addition, he changed the school curriculum to be more traditional. This focus on tradition and respect also contradicted the changes of the 1920s, and it is therefore correct to label it a 'Great Retreat'.

🖉 This essay focuses on the question and develops an answer in a thematic way. Each of the points is backed up by some information and linked clearly to the question. Nonetheless, the information is not very detailed. The use of statistics, dates and proper names would push this answer higher within Level 4.

Level 4: 19/30

Question 4

How far do you agree that Stalin's terror intensified throughout the 1930s?

■ ■ ■

A-grade answer

Throughout the years 1930–39, Stalin dominated the USSR through terror. The Great Terror (1936–38) was the highpoint in the sense that he turned his secret police on the party. Nonetheless, in terms of numbers of people killed and sent to gulags the Terror was at its most intense in the early 1930s and during the campaign against the kulaks. Finally, following Yezhov's resignation as head of the secret police, Stalin's policy of terror diminished between 1938 and 1940. Consequently, it would be wrong to argue that the Terror intensified throughout the 1930s.

Stalin's policy of terror began with the de-kulakisation campaign from 1928. Stalin sent Communists, members of the secret police and even Red Army brigades into the countryside to enforce collectivisation. The peasants, many of whom had done well under the NEP, resisted this policy and destroyed crops, livestock and machinery rather than surrender it to the new collective farms. Stalin's response was to deport large numbers of so-called kulaks to prison camps in Siberia. It is estimated that 10% of some villages were dealt with in this way. De-kulakisation led to a famine in which an estimated 10 million people perished. The government chose not to intervene in the famine, and in some areas, particularly Ukraine, there was a deliberate policy of starving the peasants into submission. The famine, which lasted from 1932 to 1934, was the most intense expression of the Terror in the sense that it claimed the most lives. Consequently, it would be wrong to argue that terror intensified, as fewer people died in the period 1934–40.

The Great Terror marked an intensification of Stalin's policy of terror in the sense that it attacked the Communist Party. During the 1920s and early 1930s, the secret police had stopped short of attacking their own party. However, following Kirov's murder in 1934, the secret police turned its attention to the Leningrad party. Having uncovered evidence of a conspiracy in Leningrad, Stalin issued his letter 'Lessons of the events connected with the evil murder of Comrade Kirov'. This argued that Trotskyites had infiltrated the party across the entire country and therefore justified the extension of terror to the Communist Party as a whole. Initially, Yagoda's secret police were not as effective as Stalin had wanted, so Yagoda was replaced with Yezhov, who introduced a new method of interrogation known as the 'conveyor belt' system. Yezhov also recruited a new generation of secret police who were willing to use their power against the old elite. Consequently, the show trials of 1936–38 marked a high point in the Terror because they destroyed high-ranking Communist officials such as Zinoviev, Kamenev and Bukharin. The Great Terror claimed a smaller number of lives than the de-kulakisation campaign, but it could be seen as more intense because it impacted on the highest levels of the Communist Party.

Stalin used terror extensively during the de-kulakisation campaign, the famine and the Great Terror. However, it did not intensify throughout the 1930s, because between 1938 and 1940 there was a marked decrease in the Terror.

🖉 This essay clearly focuses on the question. It considers the entire time period and analyses two different senses in which the terror could be said to have intensified. However, it does not specify at which point the terror was at its most intense and therefore, although it is a very strong essay, it cannot reach Level 5.

Level 4: 23/30

C-grade answer

As soon as Stalin achieved power he set about changing Russia and making it a more Communist nation. Many of his reforms were supported by the people, but some of them weren't and so he had to use terror.

One of the first policies used as part of the Great Terror was the show trials. These put his rivals on trial and showed the people that they were traitors. It allowed Stalin to discredit people like Bukharin, Zinoviev and Kamenev. They were accused of the murder of Kirov and of sabotaging the Five-Year Plans. The first show trial was the Trial of the Sixteen, which took place in 1936. It was organised by Yagoda, who Stalin said was too slack in enforcing the Great Terror. The Trial of the Seventeen in 1937 was more intense because it was organised by Yezhov, who used the 'conveyor belt' system of interrogation which forced people to confess. The Trial of the Twenty-One in 1938 was also more intense because Yezhov finally put Bukharin on trial. Bukharin was still quite popular within the Communist Party, and this shows how extreme the Terror was.

The Great Terror became more intense in the 1930s because it attacked everyone. It is estimated that under Yezhov 10% of adult males were either executed or sent to labour camps. This is much more than under Yagoda, who only killed 1,118 people in 1936. The Terror under Yezhov, which was known as Yezhovshchina, also attacked women — 5% of the total number of people terrorised were women. This shows that the Terror became more intense because under Yezhov it affected all of society, while under Yagoda it did not.

Finally, the Great Terror was very extreme in the 1930s because it attacked the party. In 1936, Stalin launched his attack on the party, claiming that it was infested with criminals who were working for Trotsky. Stalin's real reason for this attack, however, was that there were people in the party who knew about Lenin's *Testament* and about the dirty tricks Stalin had used in order to gain power. He wanted to get rid of these people and therefore he instructed Yezhov to eliminate the party's older members in order to consolidate his own power within the party and within Russia.

Overall, the Terror was extreme during the 1930s and therefore it had widespread effects on Russia's economy, society and politics.

question

This essay contains two well developed paragraphs that focus on the question. However, the fourth paragraph focuses on Stalin's reasons for initiating the Great Terror rather than the extent to which it became more intense during the 1930s. Additionally, the essay only considers the period of the Great Terror (1936–38) and therefore overlooks the full period specified by the question.

Level 3: 18/30

Question 5

How far do you agree that it was Russia's economic might that enabled it to win the Second World War?

■ ■ ■

A-grade answer

There were four main reasons why Russia was able to win the Second World War: its economic might, the bravery and hard work of its people, Stalin's pragmatic policies on the home front and the support of the Western Allies. Although economic might was an important reason for the victory, the most significant reason was the support of the Allies. This not only forced the German armed forces to fight a war on two fronts, thus restricting the military force focused on Russia, but also provided economic help in the form of the Lend-Lease scheme. This was essential in ensuring that the Soviet armed forces had food and transport.

Economic might was important in helping Russia to win the Second World War. Preparation for war had begun in 1936 under the Second Five-Year Plan, and by 1942, 50% of national income was being spent on the war. In addition, the focus on rearmament ensured that armaments production almost doubled between 1941 and 1944. During the war, Gosplan organised the relocation of Russian industry from areas under threat from the Nazis to safer areas in the east. In fact, 1,523 factories had been moved by November 1941. This ensured that Russian industry could continue to produce goods essential to the war. Economic might therefore played an important role in helping the country to win the war, because without such a strong war economy it would not have had the arms or industrial goods necessary to defeat the Germans.

The Soviet people also played an important role. For example, while many of the men were away fighting, the women made up a substantial proportion of the workforce — in some regions as many as 75% of workers were women. On farms, women were often required to perform tasks previously performed by machinery or animals. Some women were yoked to ploughs and pulled these over the fields. In the factories, workers worked for more days and longer shifts, with 7-day working weeks throughout the war and factory shifts lasting between 10 and 12 hours. In addition, workers were expected to help in the fields at night during the harvest season. The people were thus important to Russia's victory in the war because they maintained the production of agricultural and industrial goods, and ensured that the army had the supplies it needed to win the war.

Another important factor was Stalin's pragmatic domestic policies. Stalin knew that he had to keep morale high among the people. Therefore, he appealed to Russian nationalism, calling the war the 'Great Patriotic War', and stressing that soldiers were fighting for Russia rather than mentioning socialism. In addition, he stopped his persecution of the Russian Orthodox Church, inviting Metropolitan Sergei, the leader

of the church, to live in an official residence in Moscow, and promising the church greater freedom after the war. Metropolitan Sergei responded by supporting Stalin's war effort and encouraging Russians to do the same. Stalin's domestic policy increased support for the war in Russia. Importantly, this inspired greater dedication from the people, which in turn led to increased economic production.

Finally, and most importantly, the support of the Allies enabled Russia to win the Second World War. The impact of this alliance was twofold. First, the fact that Germany had to fight the Allies in the west ensured that it could not devote all of its resources to fighting Russia in the east. Russia was only fighting a war on one front and therefore had the advantage over the German troops. Secondly, from 1941, the Allies provided economic support through the Lend-Lease scheme. Although this provided only 4% of the total goods used by the USSR during the war, it was essential in terms of providing food and transport for the soldiers. For example, it provided 10% of the tanks used by the USSR in the war, 12% of the aeroplanes, and about 66% of the jeeps. In addition, American food provided 17% of the daily calories consumed by Soviet soldiers. Clearly, Allied help was more important than Russia's economic might, because the aid provided by Lend-Lease highlights important weaknesses in the Soviet economy. The economy was not mighty enough to provide food for all citizens, nor could it provide high-quality transport. Lend-Lease made up for these weaknesses and ensured that a well-fed Soviet Army could get all the way from Russia to Berlin.

Overall, the most important reason for Russia's victory in the Second World War was the support of the Allies. Russia's economic might was important, but strong as the economy was, it also had strategic weaknesses such as its inefficient farms and the low quality of complicated products such as jeeps. The hard work of the Soviet people, motivated by Stalin's renewed emphasis on patriotism and tradition, and the country's economic might were important, but Lend-Lease compensated for these potentially deadly weaknesses, and although the contribution was small in terms of value it was enormous in terms of its significance — Soviet soldiers could never have got all the way to Berlin without American jeeps.

The essay gets to the heart of the question asked and provides good analysis of Russia's economic strengths and weaknesses. It develops a sophisticated argument that although Russia's economy was mighty it had crucial weaknesses and therefore Allied help was essential for success in the war. The essay also considers a range of other factors in quite a lot of detail. The real strength of this essay is the fact that it develops a well thought-out argument that really answers the question.

Level 5: 30/30

C-grade answer

Russia's economic might was essential in helping it to win the Second World War in three ways: the production of armaments, the maintenance of industrial production, and the dedication of national income to the war effort.

First, Russia's economic might helped the country to win the Second World War because it was able to keep the production of armaments high. For example, rearmament had started under the Second Five-Year Plan in 1936 and continued through the Third Five-Year Plan. Although the Lend-Lease scheme did contribute military equipment to the war effort, overall the USSR produced 96% of the goods it used. For example, it produced 98% of the artillery, 90% of the tanks and 88% of the aeroplanes used by its armed forces in the war. Indeed, between 1941 and 1944 the production of armaments in doubled. Thus Russia's economic might, in the form of the production of armaments, helped it to win the war by ensuring that those fighting were well equipped.

Second, Russia's economic might helped the country to win the war because it was able to maintain a high level of industrial production throughout the war. Under the Third Five-Year Plan production of heavy industry had increased in preparation for war. For example, the production of coal had increased from 128 million tonnes in 1937 to 166 million tonnes in 1940. During the war, Gosplan ensured that Russian industry was moved away from the west, where the Germans were invading, and into the east, where it was safe. By 1941, 1,523 factories had been moved. This ensured that production levels could remain high. In addition, workers in industry worked 7-day weeks in order to increase the output of the factories. The raw materials produced could then be used to make the weapons needed for war.

Finally, Russia's economic might enabled it to win the war because large amounts of the national income were dedicated to the war. Under the Third Five-Year Plan spending on defence increased substantially, and by 1940, one-third of all investment went to the armed forces and military spending had more than doubled. By 1942, 50% of the USSR's national income was being spent on the war. This was significant, as it was a much higher figure than that of Germany. This shows that Russia's economic might helped it to win the war, because it was able to devote so much money to preparing for, and then fighting, the war. This enabled it to produce more weapons with which to fight the war.

This essay is well written, focused on the question, analytical and detailed. It is analytical in the sense that it considers three different ways in which Russia's economic might contributed to victory in the war. Nonetheless, the essay lacks balance, because it doesn't consider other possible explanations for success. What it does, it does well, but a greater range of factors is necessary for a higher mark in Level 4.

Level 4: 19/30